ANGER MANAGEMENT

The Complete Guide to Overcome your Anger and Stress using the Mindfulness Approach

SIMON GRANT

© **Copyright 2020 by Simon Grant - All rights reserved.**

This document is geared towards providing exact and reliable information in regard to the topic and issue covered. The publication is sold with the idea that the publisher is not required to render accounting, officially permitted, or otherwise, qualified services. If advice is necessary, legal or professional, a practiced individual in the profession should be ordered.

From a Declaration of Principles which was accepted and approved equally by a Committee of the American Bar Association and a Committee of Publishers and Associations.

In no way is it legal to reproduce, duplicate, or transmit any part of this document in either electronic means or in printed format. Recording of this publication is strictly prohibited and any storage of this document is not allowed unless with written permission from the publisher. All rights reserved.

The information provided herein is stated to be truthful and consistent, in that any liability, in terms of inattention or otherwise, by any usage or abuse of any policies, processes, or directions contained within is the solitary and utter responsibility of the recipient reader. Under no circumstances will any legal responsibility or blame be held against the publisher for any reparation, damages, or monetary loss due to the information herein, either directly or indirectly.

Respective authors own all copyrights not held by the publisher.

The information herein is offered for informational purposes solely, and is universal as so. The presentation of the information is without contract or any type of guarantee assurance.

The trademarks that are used are without any consent, and the publication of the trademark is without permission or backing by the trademark owner. All trademarks and brands within this book are for clarifying purposes only and are owned by the owners themselves, not affiliated with this document.

Table of Contents

Introduction 1

Chapter One: The Brain During Anger Episodes 5
    The Parts of the Brain that Deal with Anger 8

Chapter Two: What is Mindfulness? 13
    What Is Mindfulness? 16
    So What Else is Mindfulness? 21

Chapter Three: How Anger Affects Relationships 25
    Creating Space Between You and the Trigger of Your Anger ... 27
    Looking at the Problem from the Perspective of Others 28

Chapter Four: Looking into Your Triggers 32

Chapter Five: Introducing Mindfulness 37

Chapter Six: Exercises When Anger Arises 41
    Exercise 1 – Breathing 41
    Exercise 2 – Mindfulness Walking 42
    Exercise 3 – Mindfulness Eating 43
    Exercise 4 - Mindfulness Touch and Taste Tests 44
    Exercise 5 – Mindfulness Anger Management Exercise 45
    Exercise 5 – Work and Undesirable Tasks 46

    Exercise 6 – Empathy Exercise.. 47

Chapter Seven: Getting Back to the Basics 49
    What Does This Have To Do With A Temper?......................... 50

Chapter Eight: Using a Body Scan.. 54

Chapter Nine: The Benefits of Mindfulness Meditation 58
    Your Partner Does Something That Really Bugs You................ 60
    So Why Do People Get Angry? 61

Chapter Ten: Count and Breathe... 63
    Focused Breathing Exercise 65
    Expelling Anger Through The Breathing................................... 66
    The 4-7-8 Method of Breathing.. 67
    Alternate Nostril Breathing 67

Chapter Eleven: Preparing Yourself for Daily Meditation........... 70
    What Does This Have To Do With Meditation? 70
    Committing to Meditation.. 71
    Seating Position 72
    Mindfulness And The Environment You Meditate In................ 73
    When Should You Meditate? 74

Chapter Twelve: Mindful Meditation in Practice 75
    Why Do You Need To Be Aware Of The Breath?...................... 77
    What Can I Do If Thoughts Won't Stop?................................... 77
    What If My Sitting Position Is Uncomfortable?........................ 78
    What If I Get Interrupted While I Am Meditating? 78

Can I Meditate With Others?.. 79
Can I Meditate After Breakfast?... 79
What Does It Mean To Let Go Of Thoughts? 79
Focused Meditation.. 80

Chapter Thirteen: Letting Go Of Thoughts 81
Emotional Thoughts... 83
An Exercise in Mind Shifting.. 86

Chapter Fourteen: Letting go of Judgment and Blame 89
So How Do You Let Go of Judgment?... 89
Mindfulness and Judgment 92
Exercise in Self-Control... 94
How Blame Works 96

Chapter Fifteen: What Should You Expect of Yourself During Meditation?.. 99

Chapter Sixteen: Self-Love and Respect from Mindfulness....... 103

Conclusion... 110

References... 114

Introduction

In the world that we live in today, there is little wonder that people suffer from anger. We are fed so many stimuli that the mind is always occupied. In fact, overload would be an appropriate word to use to explain what our everyday world does to the brain. You may be multi-tasking – which incidentally doesn't work – and at the same time checking to see what alerts you have on your phone. You may be interrupted by noises in the world around you, or you may simply be angry at people you know for reasons that are pretty lame when it comes to the overall importance of life. One thing is for sure. If you continue to allow this overload, it's inevitable that you are going to experience anger and then some. Anger can result from being overwhelmed; this has so many different forms that I thought it would be worthwhile creating a book on the subject. I use mindfulness to help people with anger management and my success rate confirms the fact that it works and is something that can easily be adopted into your life.

Have you ever thought about what's going on in the brain when you are angry? Well, if so, you have come to the right place to find information. This isn't written in a complex medical way because that would add to your overload. What I have done is take the problem of anger and isolate it, explaining what's happening and why it is happening, and then have laid out alternatives for you using a system called mindfulness. You may have heard of it in passing, and perhaps you think it's a little "out there" to want to participate in, but basically, mindfulness is bringing your mind back to the present moment and being able to banish thoughts from the past or worries about the future. It's really as simple as that, but what you don't know is what's happening behind the scenes, and when you understand that a little better, you will see that it's the only way forward. It helps you to help yourself.

In fact, this kind of treatment has become so successful these days that doctors in the United Kingdom are prescribing it for people who have problems rather than putting them onto drugs that may otherwise extend their anxiety long term. The problem with drugs is that although there are continual advances being made in the field of medicine, when it comes to troubles of the mind, we know that anxiety and anxiety-related illnesses are on the rise. I would not suggest that anger is an illness, but believe me, if left unharnessed, it can become one.

Many years ago, the system of mindfulness was discovered in the United States, but there are other sources from which this practice derived. For example, we know that going back as far as before Christ, people practiced the art of meditation. Thus, they were aware of the benefits of quietening the mind at that stage. Imagine what those people would think in today's world. There is so much outside influence in our lives that I suppose the guys who came up with the new notions on mindfulness took into account the stress factor as it applied in the 20th century as opposed to stresses which may no longer be relevant to today. The practices within this book combine both the original practices and the newer practices and are designed to help you to gain control over what's going on in your mind and combat anger.

There are also areas of the book that deal with the process of anger and how it comes about. You may not know, for example, which parts of the brain are active during anger episodes and what's happening hormonally within your head, and in fact, the rest of your body. The fight or flight instinct will be explained so that at the end of reading this book, you will be in a better position to do something positive about your anger and learn to live in harmony with your thoughts, instead of being afraid of them.

Anger combines several factors, and mindfulness counters this because it makes you look inside yourself. It also makes you much more aware of other people in a more empathetic way, so that they no longer provide a stimulus for your anger. The fact is that anger is something that an individual can control given the right tools, and that's exactly what this book provides; the know how to do that. You control the health of your mind to a certain extent, and with mindfulness, you up the ante and make it possible to be totally in control of your thought patterns and the way that you react to the different circumstances that present themselves during the course of your life.

I hope that you will enjoy reading it and that it will help you on your journey toward becoming a better person. When you have combatted anger, you begin to see the world from a much more positive perspective and can enjoy your cohabitation with others in a more fruitful way. Perhaps you have tried all kinds of different remedies for anger, but this book provides sufficient information for you to deal with this on your own. You may even choose to read through it with your partner so that you are both walking the same walk, and they will be reassured that you are taking the necessary steps to curb your anger in the future.

Even though you may doubt your ability to use mindfulness as a remedy for your anger, be open-minded. It has helped so many people to go forward in their lives and to find solutions to everyday problems. Letting go of thoughts is also dealt with in the book, and although it may appear to be one of the hardest things to do, you may be surprised at how easily you can distract the mind on the side of positivity to replace angry thoughts. Maybe a journey through this book will be a fruitful one.

Chapter One

The Brain During Anger Episodes

"Angry people are not always wise."
~ **Jane Austen** – Pride and Prejudice

As you must already know, there are certain triggers that are likely to make anger happen. While the triggers are not to blame, your brain believes they are and will respond with anger when these common triggers occur. Remember, it's your perception of things externally, but it's also your brain's reaction that causes anger to be such a negative influence in your life. It's easy to point at things and say these are why I lose my temper, but the harder road is a much more long-lasting one because what you will study is what is happening in the brain and how you can counter it so that your own response to triggers changes. You know full well that some people experience what appears to be a lack of anger. They don't get phased by things. Others will snap at the slightest thing, but the basis of these triggers could be any one of the following:

Disappointment – A common trigger of anger, although disappointment is created by expectations that do not happen. You may expect your child to get good grades, but your expectations of those grades may actually be the reason that the child failed. You see, when you have expectations, you put limitations on what's acceptable to you and what is not, and anger follows disappointment in people around you, or in events that promise to be better than they actually are. The most important aspect here is your own approach. For example, if you give a gift with an expectation of receiving a gift, then you are not really giving at all. It has strings attached to it. You can avoid disappointment by simply lowering your expectations of others or even recognizing that you don't have the right to expect anything of others. When you change your approach and cut down your expectations, you will find that happiness replaces disappointment and that you are pleasantly surprised by people around you rather than being angry, and that anger is caused by disappointment.

Judgment - One of the biggest triggers of anger is judgment, which is why judgment is excluded from mindfulness. The moment you judge something, you put yourself into a position that you are not entitled to be in. You judge others. You get angry because they don't live up to your expectations or because they do not fit into your moral standards. You will find out how judgment affects you more than it affects others during the course of this book. Mindfulness encourages you to see the bigger picture or to understand that every single human being has the right to an opinion. When you look at it from a more compassionate stance, you find that there are always reasons why other people's opinions differ from your own. You will also be taught how to expand on your empathy, thus being able to place yourself into the shoes of those who you currently judge. The story isn't always as clear cut as you think it is.

Fear – If you back a wolf into a corner, what you produce in that wolf is fear. The wolf does not know how to get out of that situation, and anger will become the only way that he can deal with this fear. It's the same for human beings for a very good reason. Inside your brain, chemicals are released to help to prevent danger. The fight or flight response to life made more sense for our ancestors, because the dangers that they had to face every day may have ended their lives. However, the fight or flight response hasn't really evolved into the 21st century is a very meaningful way. Yes, it will help you when you are put in danger, but it's more likely to cause you anger and frustration because you feel trapped. This, in turn, releases certain hormones within your body, and the result of this is anger.

Rejection – Not everyone who suffers rejection answers it with anger, but some do, and there's nothing worse than feeling that you don't measure up. It's almost like being paraded in front of others and mocked; in this situation, it can stimulate the part of the brain that releases the fight or flight hormones that try and help your body to deal with what's happening. Anger comes from the frustration of knowing that you failed or from becoming a disappointment to those who matter to you. However, when you learn to deal with rejection in a new way and use it as a life lesson, you begin to develop a new way of looking at life and a better understanding of the things that are happening in your life. Mindfulness helps you to do that.

The Parts of the Brain that Deal with Anger

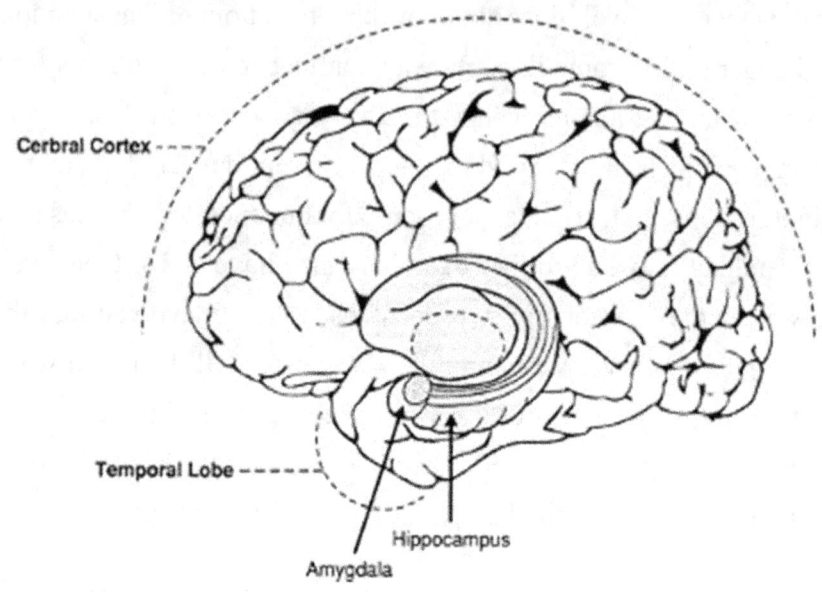

The Amygdala part of the brain is the first affected by the emotion of anger. If you talk about the things that make you feel angry, then it is this part of the brain that feels it first. It's responsible for fear and other elements in your life that may give way to anger. Do you remember how you feel when you hear a dentist's drill? Or perhaps you feel a horrid sensation when you hear chalk on a blackboard. These memories that pertain to fear or association with negative things will be dealt with in this area of the brain. It is also a center for the release of hormones to counterbalance or ready the body to counteract that fear.

There are all kinds of things triggered within the brain when this section senses danger. For example, your heart rate may increase, and your blood pressure rises. You may find that your pupils are dilated and that your natural metabolism increases. The reason for this is the self-preservation of the body, but since we really don't need to be that alert in everyday life, it can also result in anger because of all the changes happening within the body and the release of hormones to make you quicker and more receptive to what's going on around you. The great thing about anatomy is that there are ways these days to measure this area, and IMR scans have come in very useful to determine how active this part of the anatomy is when people are doing such things as meditation. What does that have to do with mindfulness? You will have to wait to get that answer, but you will be impressed. For the time being, it's enough to know that the triggers of anger all start in this area of the brain when it responds to stimuli.

The hippocampus area of the brain is the part of the brain responsible for sorting out important memories. For example, if you have a fear of snakes, then this part of the brain will indicate to the brain that the fear presents a danger when you see a snake. It recalls all the things you consider important, and it does that by monitoring your reaction to different things during the course of your life. This will then trigger the amygdala, which is close in proximity to do something to help you to counter that danger. When you control your responses to stimuli in your life through mindfulness, you re-educate the part of the brain that deals with fear, anger, rejection, and all of the negative impacts they may have in your life.

So the cycle begins. The hippocampus tells the amygdala to release hormones, increases your blood pressure, and prepares you for battle.

However, this can also prepare you for anger, if faced by a situation that your brain knows you respond to in anger. Of course, the Big Brother – the hippocampus – is someone you can't hide from because it cleverly devises away in each individual where it can prepare that individual for any kind of danger that is perceived, and that includes your responses of anger.

So if the body is working against you, how can you change it? The fact is that you can adapt your responses so that your hippocampus remembers different things. If you take the example of fear or phobia, gradual introduction to those things that you fear, under the medical supervision, of course, can help you to get rid of phobias so that your brain does not throw off the alarm bells. Well, it's pretty much the same for your anger triggers. When you learn mindfulness, you retrain the brain so that it doesn't respond in the same way, and if you want proof of this, as you probably will do, take the example of an American neuroscientist. This YouTube video (How Meditation Can Reshape Our Brains: Sara Lazar at TEDx Cambridge 2011) is out there for anyone to see and was made by a qualified neuroscientist who didn't think that there would be any difference to the brain if you practiced mindfulness. Dr. Sara Lazar, with all of her studies on the anatomy of the human brain, did not believe that mindfulness or meditation could make a difference in the way that the brain responds to certain triggers. However, she was in for a shock. Having taken MRI examinations of brains, she was able to see quite clearly from her own experience that the shape of the mind could change and that the experience of mindfulness would indeed make her more tolerant, compassionate, and empathetic.

In fact, this video is so impressive that I use it with students who are learning mindfulness; it reminds them of why they are doing it and to show them that they too can experience the same inner peace that Dr. Lazar found following her own mindfulness experience. The shape of the brain alters during the course of a lifetime, and your own input can alter it too; this gave rise to many people being convinced that mindfulness does have a role to play in changing your anger factor and can eliminate the negativity you see as part of your everyday life. This changing of the shape of the brain was particularly relevant in the case of people who meditated on a regular basis.

During a normal anger episode, the hippocampus tells the amygdala to release hormones into the body and to prepare the body for fight or flight. But it doesn't have to do this. If you are already programmed to handle life without anger, then the hippocampus will instead see your pattern of thinking as being normal and will not trigger those reactions. Thus, you don't get worked up and angry by things that may have previously worked to make you very angry indeed. It's a question of training and also repetitive responses that allow the hippocampus to change its view about whether you need to get angry or not. If you want to blame anyone for your anger, blame the hippo because really, it's his fault, but it's you who created the memories that the hippocampus holds dear, so you need to move forward and teach it other ways to see the situations that happen in the future.

This book was written for that specific purpose to help you to be able to control the way that the mind responds to life. In the next chapters,

I will be showing you methods to help you to do just that. The associations made by the hippocampus can be changed, and that's what makes it all interesting. A fear of heights can be overcome by gradual exposure so that the hippocampus no longer relates fear with coming into a situation that would normally have stimulated fear. The fear factor is lessened, and the hippocampus doesn't respond in the same way because it knows that you have experienced less fear. You overwrite what's stored there by the changes that you make in your life, and over the course of a lifetime many things can change their importance to you. What you can depend upon is the hippocampus to appreciate these changes and register them.

Chapter Two

What is Mindfulness?

"Our life is shaped by our mind.
We become what we think."
Buddha

When I am explaining this to students, I merely state that mindfulness is being aware of this very moment. Of course, they have questions, and many of them, but the most common ones are about what mindfulness actually is. It's okay being told about something, but you do need to trust it to make it part of your everyday life, do indeed need to know what mindfulness is if you are going to practice it. Here's a list of what it isn't which is also useful in determining what makes mindfulness work:

- It is not concentration

- It is not trying to do something

- It is not a make or break exercise, but one that you practice daily

- There is no race to get it right

- It's not like you measure yourself by your achievement

Let me explain these things further. For example, in this competitive world, we are accustomed to concentrating or trying to do things that matter. Well, mindfulness just is a state of mind and is balanced out by breathing exercises. You can't try to concentrate on it because once you do, you lose the mindfulness aspect of it. For example, you may be asked not to think at all, so if you are concentrating, then you are immediately breaking the rule of simply being in that moment. No concentration is needed, and concentration can destroy mindfulness. Instead of this, you simply place your mind into the moment. The breathing that you do is in a series of counts so that you are aware of what your body is doing while it is breathing. Normally, you take all of this for granted. After all, if we didn't breathe, we wouldn't survive, but the kind of breathing you learn with mindfulness is purposeful and much deeper than your average day to day breathing. Do you know how big your lungs are? Probably not, but most people don't use the full capacity of their lungs when they breathe. Normal shallow breathing is what we are accustomed to. When you do the exercises later on in the book, you will learn to breathe in a certain way that is mindful as opposed to thinking about breathing and then doing it. Concentration takes away the spontaneity of mindfulness, and it's all about being present, rather than having your mind elsewhere.

The things to be conscious of during mindfulness are your own senses. Because our minds are so busy with other things, these days, we pay little attention to our sense of sight, touch, hearing, smell, etc. and these become very important to mindfulness. Imagine if a little like going back to basics and starting over. In the real world that stresses and angers you, there are so many things that play on your mind and if you imagine these as cardboard boxes stored in your head, left half-open, there's very little wonder why you cannot control the emotions that keep popping out of these boxes. Mindfulness helps you to close the boxes and replace them with inner peace so that the anger doesn't come as an automatic response to life. It's very clever, and it actually works very well indeed. It works on the areas of the brain that are responsible for your responses to life. You already know that the hippocampus stores your memories, but what makes every individual special is the fact that each hippocampus stores different things because we are all unique, and all have unique actions and memories.

When you TRY to do something, you expect to have achievement at the end of it. With mindfulness, there is no judgment of self, so you don't have that same restraint. You are not trying to achieve anything other than temper control. Thus, during your mindfulness sessions, you would let go of those perceptions and simply go with the flow of the lesson or the home session, not trying to do anything, but simply learning to be at that moment. That's pretty hard at first for people who have been educated to think before taking actions, but it is doable, and once you learn to do it, you have control over much more than just your anger. Have you ever watched a grandmother's knitting? The chances are that she is able to do that without even giving it a thought because it's become automatic. It is this automation that you seek when you go into mindfulness. You simply are, rather than attempting anything in particular.

When you exercise, you have expectations, such as you may tell yourself that you will skip for a set amount of time, or that you will do so many repetitions of exercises within your exercise regime. Apart from setting aside a small amount of time each day to incorporate mindfulness, it's not a sport, so you don't have to have expectations of achieving anything. Some people find that part of mindfulness very difficult to cope with, but throughout this book, you will learn how to do just that. It's not a race. There are no winners or heroes. You are simply exercising a different way of breathing and perhaps even a different way to feed positivity to the hippocampus so that your responses change, and you are calmer within yourself.

What about the measurement of your achievement? Well, all I can say on this score is that you don't need to measure your achievement because you will feel it. You will be less anxious and more capable of being understanding and kind toward others, and thus your anger management will be in control. You will also be happier and more capable of feeling positivity, and that's a wonderful side effect of mindfulness. You see more and appreciate more and are no longer so busy that you cannot stop to smell the roses. Does it mean you'll achieve less? In fact, it means you will achieve more because you are more aware of what you can and can't do and more inclined to try new things.

What Is Mindfulness?

If you go back in time to a time before Jesus was born, sages and wise men practiced meditation and mindfulness to try to enhance their spiritual understanding of the world. Of course, there are not many written testaments from this time, but we do know that the original Buddha who lived several centuries before Christ, was taught this skill so it must have been in existence way back in time in the form of meditation. However, since the western world sees things differently to other cultures, it occurred to Jon Zabat-Zin of the University of Massachusetts that there was some grounding to the theory that mindfulness was relevant in this day and age and that it could be used to help people find peace of mind and to handle stress and even anger. It was based on eastern philosophy and much of the teachings of Buddhists and Zen Buddhism, but with a slight difference – it related more to people in the western world. Although you may be concerned about getting involved in something "Zen," you won't actually be asked to do anything of a religious nature. You will simply be taught a different approach to life – one that will make your life a lot easier. The mindfulness that we know of today is modified in that although it uses the original premise, it reflects 21st-century life and is probably needed more now than in any time in our history, because of the noise of the world that we live in and the perpetual invasion of our minds by advertisements, stress, social expectations, etc. Our idea of success these days is measured by earnings and what we own, and it shouldn't be because quite frankly, being rich doesn't make the rich man happier or more fulfilled personally. It may make his life a little easier, but you only have to look at examples of people who are rich who are struggling with identities, such as Prince William in the UK or people whose fortunes have actually made them reclusive.

Classes began, and the kind of exercises that people took part in exercised that excluded the feeling of judgment. Judgment is always going to produce negative emotions, and these add to the stress, so the lack of judgment was imperative to the process of mindfulness. Simply to be in the moment and to be aware of the moment was the premise that was used to make it relevant to people of all religions, so that they could gain a better quality of life. I think that regardless of your religion, it helps you to understand all of the mindfulness practices to know what Buddhism is based upon. It's not a religion per se, it is a philosophy, so even people from your religion or any religion can practice it. The Buddhist philosophy came into being when Prince Siddhartha Gautama, who was born to a wealthy royal family, discovered for the first time how mankind suffered. He had lived a privileged life, protected from all bad things by his father the King, and when he ventured into the world, he was shocked to see how people age, how they suffer, and how suffering affects mankind in general. Although this is a story that dates back a very long time, he meditated on finding solutions to mankind's suffering and came up with guidelines for life that would improve the way that people lived. These formed the basis of Buddhism from a very simplistic viewpoint, but it's all that you need to know at this stage in order to understand mindfulness. The eightfold path was the path that he suggested people follow in order to limit their own suffering, and he was right:

BUDDHA'S Noble Eightfold Path

1. Right view
2. Right Intentions
3. Right mindfulness
4. Right concentration
5. Right effort
6. Right speech
7. Right action
8. Right livelihood

Right View – was looking at life in the right way.

Right Intentions – meaning honorable intentions

Right Mindfulness – meant being aware of life around you.

Right concentration – simply meant being instead of being absent.

Right effort – Putting in the work that you need to put in.

Right speech – not saying things that hurt yourself or others.

Right action – doing the right thing.

Right livelihood – although this was aimed toward people of the time, it meant that your work should not be exploiting others or unethical.

The foundation of the Buddhist philosophy began here with these simple paths, but whether you take them into your life or not determines how much unhappiness you experience as a result. All of these things can be related to your anger. For example, if you break any of these ways, what you are doing is encouraging negativity into your life, and negativity itself feeds the mind with negative thoughts that can lead to anger. They are fairly common-sense rules that anyone can apply to their lives, and even if you choose to stay in the same job and mix with the same people who may make you angry, it will change the way that you look at life, and thus the anger factor will be conquered by starting to see life in a different way. These principles are so easy to relate to within the modern era and are effective in all societies, and we can also relate to them in the western world. What's complicated about having the right approach to life, being aware of what we say, being aware of our actions, and acting in a moral way? These are all parts of the foundation of Buddhism but were simply conceived to help people in general – whether Buddhist or not – to improve their lives. Mindfulness takes all of this into account and allows you the freedom to explore the elements of your life to an extent that you are aware of what's going on inside you rather than merely concentrating on external values and external changes.

So What Else is Mindfulness?

One of the things that students find the hardest to accept is that mindfulness places you at this current moment in time and that thoughts of the past or worries about the future don't come into play. I want you to try a short experiment. We know that you have thousands of thoughts in the process of a day. Now sit in a chair and make yourself comfortable. Close your eyes for a moment and try to stop your thoughts. Breathe in and out and see how long you last before thoughts come flooding into your mind, and makings chains of thoughts appear. The problem is that a human mind is geared toward negativity for self-protection, but the fact is that we don't live in those times when we need all this negative thought. We are not in imminent danger every moment of our lives, so there's no need to keep grasping at negative thoughts to try to get through this moment in time.

Your thought processes are only geared in this way until YOU make changes, and mindfulness helps you to do that because the word mindful means being aware, rather than how our grandparents taught us to be mindful of our manners. It's all about awareness, and that's what will help you to overcome your anger, as I will demonstrate in the chapters to come.

Write down in a journal how long you lasted without thinking anything. It won't have been very long at all, but as you progress through the book, your mindfulness will increase, and your experience will become better. The whole point is that you came to this book to find answers. The answers are there, but you have to want to find them, and you can only do this by practicing mindfulness on a regular basis. I will show you how. For the time being, when you find a gap in your day, simply close your eyes and try to empty those thoughts by breathing and being aware of your senses.

Mindfulness includes moments in your day when you actually observe life instead of always allowing what the Buddhists call the "monkey mind" to be in charge of what you are thinking. It's very easy to let thoughts run away with you, but mindfulness will help to pull you back into the moment so that you learn when those thoughts are appropriate and when they are not. Mindfulness will help you to feel calmer. It will help you to enjoy your life and your relationships better but most of all it will take away much of the anger that you feel because you will be more compassionate toward others and understand that there are many perspectives in life and sometimes your perspectives do not line up with other people's, but that's no reason to show anger. When you accept that life is forever changing and see the perspectives of others, you also understand that what makes you angry at this moment can become history in the next moment. Mindfulness takes a step into your life when you let it, and by using it as your guide for life, you can avoid placing yourself in the judgmental situation of being angry because of all of the triggers that have made you angry in the past.

Now try it again, and instead of trying to think about nothing, simply think of your breathing. Hear the breath come into your body and feel it fill the upper abdomen. Then breathe out and keep on doing this to see how long it takes before other thoughts invade your headspace.

You can get over this, and you can move on from anger. In fact, if a loved one is suggesting that anger is a problem, show that loved one that you are making an effort by letting them see the book. It will help to reassure them, but it will do more than that. It will keep you committed to the process of learning to use mindfulness to counter your anger.

During the course of the next week, try to be what we call observant. That means looking at the things you usually take for granted. For example, how does it make you feel when your partner does certain things? It may be the fact that your partner presents you with a great meal or simply a little habit that your partner has that makes you feel good about life. Explore all of the elements of nature that make you feel good. Feed the birds if you want to, or simply observe the seasons through what the plants are doing. We spend a great deal of our time focusing on thoughts that really don't matter in the grand scheme of things, and ignore those that do matter - the weather, the cloud formations, the smell of the flowers, the nature around us, or the things we can feel with our senses. When was the last time you actually smelled something fantastic? Go over it and remember it. Your body was built in a certain way to help you to enjoy life more. Your ears, for hearing the most wonderfully uplifting sounds, your eyes, to see all the colors of the world around you. Your taste buds were invented to help you to enjoy tastes and textures. Your fingertips are able to distinguish between velvet and plastic, but what 21st-century life has done is taken all of those things for granted and put them on the back shelf in favor of what we call progress.

Mindfulness helps you to get this back again and to understand in a better way how your body interacts with the world around it.

Over the course of the next few chapters, you are going to become involved in learning all about mindfulness, but for the time being, consciously make yourself more aware of the environment in which you live by the use of your senses. This will help your intuition. It will help your positivity, and it will certainly make you feel something other than anger.

Chapter Three

How Anger Affects Relationships

"Anger doesn't solve anything.
It builds nothing, but it can destroy everything."
~ Anon

I need to include this chapter because anger has consequences. You cannot say something in anger and expect others to forget it in a hurry. The reason? What you say hurts the people around you, and when you keep making hollow promises that you will try better, unfortunately, you have also lost the trust of those people who matter to you. Anger comes out in all kinds of ways, but the consequences are clear:

- You say things that you later regret
- You have to live with the consequences of what you say
- You can never take things back once they are spoken
- You may hurt people you love by simply using anger as a response

Now let's look at the advantages of anger control and mindfulness:

- People will trust you more with their feelings

- People around you will be open and communicative

- People will not fear you

- People will be able to see a compassionate human being instead of a grouch

The mind is not working at its most rational when you show anger. It's like a kettle that has been near to boiling, and the only way that you can move forward from it is to display your anger just as the boiling kettle expels vapor and lots of it. However, there are other ways forward. At this point in time, you don't know those answers, which is why you have come here in the first place. I want you to try to do something for me, and this exercise may be personally painful.

I want you to close your eyes and think back to something that someone said to you that hurt you to the core. While we may never have to go back to those moments of hurt again, it is important that you feel the anger that was directed toward you. You should feel its impact and feel the hurt associated with it because that's what your anger does to other people, whether you are aware of it or not. The reason I want you to do this is that you need to be reminded about how anger hurts and can continue to hurt many years into the future. I know personally that things my parents said to me as a child still have an impact now, and perhaps that's what your anger is doing to people you love.

Jackie was an only child. She was afraid to venture away from the constraints that her parents put on her. She wanted to become a dancer but knew that her father would never approve of that. In fact, she had broached the subject once, and he had become angry and abusive about it. Thus, she never brought that up again. Jackie went through most of her life, resenting the fact that she could never do what she had her heart set on. She wasn't talking about disco dancing. She was talking about a career as a ballerina, but now it was too late for that ever to happen. All of her life, she had bowed down to the wants of her father because she was afraid of him to the extent that none of her own wishes in life were relevant. However, the resentment lasted a lifetime. Anger can cut into the very soul, and although you may not mean it to do that, careless words at the wrong time may just be killing off someone else's dreams, and you may never even be aware that you are guilty of it.

With the help of mindfulness, you will learn not to inflict your anger on others, but instead learn to contain it and come back with reasonable responses that help to resolve situations rather than making them worse. Some of the ways in which you can harness anger are the following:

Creating Space Between You and the Trigger of Your Anger

Often when anger happens, all of your body gears up to the release of hormones that make you a little irrational. When you feel yourself getting angry, one of the best things you can do is learn to say, "I cannot deal with this at this moment in time but will be happy to clear up any misunderstandings later." Then walk away. Fueling your anger is like throwing petrol onto a fire. It never makes you feel good, and it makes people around you feel afraid. Thus, if you put distance between you and the source of your anger, you are more capable of looking at things from the perspective of distance and making sense of whatever it was that made you angry. This is the first line of approach when anger happens. Sometimes one-upmanship makes you want to have your say, but at the end of the day, does it really matter to the bigger picture of your life?

This space that you create between yourself and your anger is healthy, and you should try to concentrate on other things. Take a walk in the park. Go for a drive and simply look around you, being aware of the countryside. Don't add fuel to the anger, but simply let go of it until you can come back with answers that are logical and that do not involve any kind of anger at all.

Looking at the Problem from the Perspective of Others

If your child does something terribly wrong, the chances are that the child was trying to gain the approval of his/her peers. The problem here is that you are the adult, and you find it hard to understand why your child would do something that seemed so childish and unreasonable. The fact is that your child needed to. It's as simple as that. Children need to make mistakes so that they learn from them. The chances are that your child is already remorseful about what was done. Your anger won't make the child feel any better about what they did. It will merely add fuel to the fire already going on in his mind. What you need to understand is why your child did what they did, and you can only do that by using perspective, examining what was done and why you believe the child would justify it, from his perspective. When we take judgment out of the picture, as we do with mindfulness, you get to feel empathy which doesn't mean you let your child get away with anything the child chooses to do, but you learn to discuss what happened and why and come up with acceptable solutions rather than punishments that make your child afraid of you. Anger doesn't cut it. YOU are the adult. You need to lead by example.

I can give you a case history here of a father whose children were physically afraid of him. It was his habit to deal with his kids by taking his belt off and beating them. This showed absolutely no empathy at all and didn't make the child stop misbehaving. However, it did make the child grow up with disrespect for his father. If you don't want that to be the response of your children, you need to change your attitude from anger to anger management, and we are about to introduce you to mindfulness, which will help you to do just that. The other way that the boy's life could have gone would be that he may have repeated his father's anger with his own children, simply because he knew no other way. There are two ways that kids go. They abhor the treatment they were given and learn to be better than the example they are given, or they believe it's the normal response of an adult to child misbehavior, which it isn't, and go on the repeat that with their own children.

I already talked about the consequences of anger, but the long-term consequences are far more severe and touch more lives than you may imagine. Anger is destructive. It can cause rifts in relationships. It can cause child damage that can last a lifetime, and it's never going to be the right answer when it comes to the problems that face a family on a day to day basis. Anger makes problems worse. The case I talked about above was a real case, and the psychological damage wasn't limited to the child. The wife of the person in question was also affected for years after the event and lost respect for her husband. Anger will do that, and the damage that it does can live in the minds of those who experience it for many years afterward. It is time to acknowledge that you have a problem and start to deal with it, and I will help you if you allow me to.

You may think that anger only affects those who are being chastised, but in fact, it has a negative impact on you as well. You may not know it, but little by little, you break down that self-respect element of being you, and when you do that, make yourself more miserable and harder for anyone to get on with.

I don't want to dwell too much on anger, but I do want to emphasize that your anger is misdirected – no matter who it is aimed at. Anger makes you less of a person, and the whole world can see that, and at some time or another, it's going to make you feel inferior and incapable of having decent relationships with people. If you are the sort to snap at others, mindfulness will help you to do that. The other offshoot of anger is that it leads to a negative mindset, and that comes out as anxiety, and sometimes depression. Even if you have not yet suffered from either, be aware that letting those hormones play hell with your body on a regular basis will eventually take its toll. It's hard work for the heart. It's hard for the blood pressure, and blood pressure contributes to your physical health. Strokes can be a consequence as can cancer or even heart disease. Thus, keeping everything under your own control will help you to live longer as well as having a happier coexistence with people around you.

I will show you ways to replace anger throughout this book, and that will help your relationships with your family, your kids, your colleagues, and anyone who crosses your path. You must remember at all times that anger hurts people, and you are not exempt from this. It's like self-harm without the razor blades. If you begin to think of it in this way, you will be even more inclined to try the mindfulness exercises that are outlined in this book and become a better person in the process. Angry words do indeed have consequences, and it isn't just you who will have to live with those consequences.

Write down the things that have made you angry and trace back who may have been affected by the anger that you displayed. It may surprise you. The fact is that anger is emotions out of control, and when they get that bad, everyone around you avoids you or tries to comply with your wishes, but no one really respects you for your angry state. It's certainly not something to be proud of or to aspire to. When you remove anger from your life, you are able to see a better person when you look into the mirror; you know that you have learned compassion and you know that you can be a much better friend to those who may have been wary of you in the past.

Chapter Four

Looking into Your Triggers

"Explain your anger instead of expressing it, and you will find solutions, rather than arguments."

~ Anon

For the next week, I want you to take note of all the things that trigger your anger. Instead of allowing that trigger to work, stop, breathe, and write down what triggered that feeling of anger. Carry a notebook so that you can keep records of your own behavior. The reason that I need you to do this is so that you can recognize your own weakness in responding in this way to certain events in your life. Perhaps someone made you angry while you were driving. What you have to start to look at is the situation as it really is, rather than simply from your own perspective. You never know anyone else's circumstances, and perhaps the person who annoyed you had a reason for doing so. The fact that you judged it in such a way as to be angry is your problem, and this is what you need to change. Perhaps the driver was so inexperienced that they made a mistake. It doesn't matter if no one was hurt. What matters is your judgment of the situation, which led to your anger. Take away judgment and anger doesn't happen. It is as simple as that. Compassion goes a long way toward understanding alternative actions that are more acceptable. I will give you an example of what I need you to write down and analyze.

What triggered my anger? – Someone was driving badly.

How did you respond? – I beeped the horn and shook my fist at her.

Potential consequences of anger. In this case, the girl driving may have been scared by the sound of the beep, and may have been intimidated by the shaking of your fist. Thus, you don't add anything to the situation except potential danger and lack of thought for a relatively inexperienced driver. The potential consequences of your actions could have been an accident. Would it have been worth it? Many unfortunate things happen as a consequence of anger, so you need to look at the overall picture of your anger and try to make notes of what the consequences are. The problem here is that you may not realize the consequences that are suffered by those to whom you have shown your anger.

Every time that your anger is triggered breathe in and breathe out and think about what triggered your anger, how you felt, how you would normally respond, how you responded having held your anger back. You will find that the alternative is always going to produce better results than anger does.

There is a trick that you can use to get rid of your anger temporarily. I want you to breathe into the count of eight, and breathe out to the count of ten. While you are doing this, you are helping your body to normalize itself. The blood pressure goes back to normal. The heartbeat goes down, and your temper subsides. Keep breathing in this way, even if you have to excuse yourself from the situation for a moment while you do this. While you are breathing, bring yourself into the moment by observing things around you like the sky, the trees, the ambiance, and everything that is touched by your senses. What you are doing is enabling yourself to calm down, and when you are calmer, your response to feeling angry will be a lot more fruitful.

William walked in the park when he was angry as he found that what happened was that the energy he expended during walking allowed the thoughts to go down from the boiling point and begin to mellow within his mind. He also found that often he found solutions to problems by simply letting go of them for a moment. An example here is hypothetical, but the problems that you have in one moment may be completely different in the next, and this scenario is being used to explain that. Suppose that William went to the park to walk off his problems. He still has negative feelings for his wife, but at the same time, he knows that the energy he burns off from walking will calm it. In the meantime, while thinking something nasty about his wife, he sees a child about to fall into the canal. What he does next is amazing. He sees that the danger of the child is more important than the anger he feels toward his wife, and he saves the child. That's how fleeting angry thoughts can be. One moment, you may want to hit someone, but the next moment, you may find that something comes up that is more important than the urge to hit. These are transient thoughts that come and go, and you need to understand how fickle they are. William recalled going home to his wife after that rescue and feeling very grateful that it wasn't his kid that had fallen into the canal. His anger was replaced by gratitude for something far more important to him.

Let's see what anger does. You get angry with someone and shout. Anger doesn't stop there. Anger creates fear, and it creates a situation much worse than the original problem. When a man gets angry at his son for telling lies, it is likely that the cause of the lies is that the child is afraid of his father, and it is the father's anger that makes the child lie to him in the first place. I can cite cases where this has been the situation, and it helps no one. It doesn't help the child to discuss things with his father, and it doesn't help the father because he believes everything the child says is lies. The long-term damage that is caused by anger also makes it a fruitless activity. Now think how else a parent could have dealt with the situation. Calmly talking to the child about his activities without fear being involved may not give you answers that you want to hear, but at least those answers won't be as a result of fear of your temper. You need to accept that we all see the world from different perspectives but that you are the adult and it is your job to serve up an example; to not lose your temper and discuss situations openly and honestly without shouting or lashing out.

Your triggers could be anything. Everyone is different. For example, I am not keen on stupidity. I am not keen on people being dishonest, but instead of getting angry about these things, I make a choice – I walk away if I can't make any difference to the situation, or I discuss it if I believe that discussion can help my own understanding. Over the next week, as you write down what triggered anger, write down your usual way of responding and then reframe the situation and come up with more acceptable responses that would make the situation better, rather than making the situation worse. All the time that you are doing this, remember the roll-off from anger or the difference it will make to the people who are involved in the angry situation; that's the bit that angry people often forget, in an attempt to get their point across. Is it worth it? Is anger ever worth it? The answer is firm no. In fact, if you can win what you want out of life without making people afraid, it's likely to be much more rewarding for everyone.

Think of yourself as going through the motions of understanding your own anger. This helps considerably because when you observe your own actions and control them, you take a much better stance and are likely to find that life becomes easier, but that problems of this nature that make you angry minimize. The best thing about this is what happens to your stress levels, as they begin to become more manageable. Many people revert to medications when they are stressed, and you may even find if you are one of them, that you don't need these as much as you do now, once you have control of your blood pressure and the manner in which you address anger. However, make sure that you have appropriate blood tests and doctor's approval before you decide to stop meditations for high blood pressure. This is extremely important as high blood pressure isn't the issue here. It's the anger that causes it, and while you may feel better for having calmed your anger, there may be underlying reasons why your doctor has you on these medications in the first place.

Chapter Five

Introducing Mindfulness

"We waste so much energy trying to cover up who we are when beneath every attitude is the want to be loved, and beneath every anger is a wound to be healed and beneath every sadness is the fear that there will not be enough time." **Mark Nepo**

You may be a little skeptical about mindfulness, and that's normal. It's not your normal state of mind, and it may be difficult at first to start to introduce it to your life. In this exercise, I would like you to make yourself a cup of your favorite drink. While you are making it, concentrate completely on what you are doing and try to banish thoughts that come to you that are not relevant to this moment. Enjoy the heat of the cup in your hands. Enjoy the aroma of the drink. Enjoy the first sip that hits your taste buds, but instead of just swallowing like you normally would, let the drink sit on your tongue for a moment so that you can thoroughly enjoy the taste. Sit down to drink so you can relax. The whole point of the exercise is to show you what mindfulness is. It's a matter of being present in this moment so that everything that is happening in your mind is relevant to this very moment in time. For example, there may be birds outside the window or clouds in the sky. The sun may be shining, or it may be raining. Observe the world with all of your senses, and every time that you find yourself thinking about things that are not relevant to this moment, stop yourself and go back to being at this moment.

It may seem like a lot of fuss to you, but you need to fight off those irrelevant thoughts that go through your mind so that you can appreciate everything about the moment that you are in. When you worry about the future, or you fret about something that happened a day ago, a week ago or even in the last hour, you are not living in this moment, but are living in retrospect. This adds unopened cardboard boxes of thoughts in your mind so that your mind is filled up with things that may even trigger your anger. Thus, learning to do this will help you to switch back to this moment when you need to calm yourself and start observing things around you so that you feel calmer and more relaxed.

I won't teach you meditation for this moment in time but am merely demonstrating how you can control what happens in your mind and see these thoughts as invasive. Imagine them as images that you see in a passing train, and one moment they are there, and then they are gone. Troubled thoughts don't have to make up part and parcel of your every waking moment. They all have their time and now is not that time. When people talk about mindfulness, their first question is, "Does this mean that I am avoiding problems by pushing those thoughts aside?" and the answer is no. All problems that you face in your life have to be dealt with at some time in one way or another. I am not asking you to forget those thoughts, but to put them to aside for the moment. They are not appropriate for your mindfulness practice.

What people do not appreciate at the beginning of learning mindfulness is that it can help you to get yourself into a state where your mind is calmer and more logical and will deal with those problems in a much calmer way because of what you have learned. It is not avoidance at all. It is simply strengthening up your responses to anything that happens in life so that you have the ability to deal with it without using anger or resorting to anger.

Another situation that may cause anger is frustration. You want to get something done, but all of the things that are happening are stopping you. You can't be in control of the actions of others. Let me give you an example. You wanted more than anything in the world to purchase something special for a gift and wanted it to get there on time. Having found that gift, the company that provides the gift goes under, and you don't have any way to get hold of anyone. It can make you very frustrated and even angry, but this anxiety is what leads to anger, and that's exactly what mindfulness will help you to stem. Instead of rushing in "bull at a gate," you will be able to calmly approach the problems that happen in your life and find solutions without resorting to anger.

Mindfulness can also help you as and when you find anger rearing its ugly head because there are certain breathing exercises you can use that will help you to overcome the fight or flight responses of your body. That response will be to fight when it encounters things that usually make you angry, i.e., your triggers, but by recognizing those triggers and responding differently over time, you can change the response held in the hippocampus to a more favorable and acceptable response; that way, you won't always equate anger or danger with situations such as those that now make you angry.

The introduction of mindfulness into your life doesn't mean you are restricted to using it at specific times. Mindfulness goes with you through your life and is your help and rescue when you feel that something has made you angry. Thus, with the exercises in the next chapter, you will be able to overcome the anger and harness it into something much more constructive. You will also be able to use mindfulness yourself out of choice when you find that you have a few moments to center your mind upon doing that. Mindfulness goes with us through our lives. For example, I responded to someone else's anger yesterday by reminding myself that the world is a beautiful place. The trees, the sky, and the sea were all close by, and the argument someone was trying to pick with me wasn't important enough to take away my mindfulness of the good things that surrounded me. When they found that they could not wind me up, they soon stopped their angry approach and started to talk about problems that I could help them with instead.

Chapter Six

Exercises When Anger Arises

*"The mind is a flexible mirror.
Adjust it to see a better world."*
Amit Ray

Mindfulness means jumping back into the moment. Whatever made you angry is now in the past, and moments of your life pass so quickly that you can experience highs and lows, anxiety and relaxation, anger, and calm, but when you use mindfulness, you control the feelings. For a moment, I want you to try the following exercises. Try these at a time when you are not stressed to do something else, but can give the exercises plenty of practice, because these will become your go-to exercises to help you to overcome anxiety and anger.

Exercise 1 – Breathing

If your first response to anger is deep breathing, you are less likely to lose your cool. However, this must be controlled breathing. The reason for this is that the purpose of this type of breathing is to bring down your blood pressure and slow your heart so that you are no longer stressed by the situation that you have found yourself in. Thus, although you are only practicing this breathing at the moment, it should be your go-to exercise whenever you find that you are in a situation that may create anger in your mind. Human beings do not use the majority of their lung capacity when they breathe, and deep breathing helps to get the sympathetic nervous system into action doing all of the jobs that it needs to do within the body.

Thus, for this exercise, please sit with your back straight on a fairly comfortable chair. Your hands can be placed on your lap, and your head should be slightly bowed. Now breathe in, and as you breathe in, count to 8 and feel the air going into your upper abdomen. Hold the breath for a moment and breathe out to the count of ten. The exhale is always longer than the inhale, and you may even find that you have to work up toward these counts. The breathing should be inhaling via your nostrils and exhaling through the mouth or your nose.

While you are breathing, try to concentrate all of your mental energy on the breathing, and if your thoughts wander elsewhere, bring yourself back to the counting. It is suggested that you do this exercise when you rise in the morning before you have your breakfast, but you need to know that you can also use it at any time during the day when you feel that your anxiety level is getting higher. The breathing helps to control the flow of oxygen within your body, and this will help you to stay calm.

Exercise 2 – Mindfulness Walking

If you are in a work situation, the chances are that you will be filled with energy and when you lose your temper that gets rid of mental energy, but there's a much more constructive way to do this. In this case, go outside or find a corridor where you can walk up and down. You have probably seen people walking up and down or in circles when they are thinking, and in this case, it's not just a case of walking. It's a case of getting your breathing in rhythm with your movements.

Breathe in as you lift your foot from the ground and notice the movement of your leg and your foot, then breathe out as you move your foot forward and place it onto the ground. One of the benefits of this type of exercise is that you are expelling energy, and by concentrating on your breathing and movement, you are letting go of the anxiety and anger. It's a great practice to do when you are anxious before a meeting or even going to an interview that really matters to you because it calms your mind and allows you to approach that situation more calmly.

If you enjoy this form of mindfulness, you may be a good candidate for yoga since this is breathing together with the movement of the body and helps you to become more flexible and mobile. It also helps you develop the ability to control the thought processes to get rid of negativity.

Exercise 3 – Mindfulness Eating

When you are on the go, the chances are that you eat on the go, and that's really bad for your digestive system. Having digestive problems can also affect your mood. If you haven't ever linked the two elements, it's time you did. If you eat your food mindlessly and don't even chew your food correctly before you swallow it, the chances are that you will give yourself indigestion, and you may even contribute to acid reflux as well as bodily discomfort later in the day. This isn't going to help your mood. As part of your anger management course, I would like you to try mindful eating. If you have a cold lunch that you have brought to work, then try to make a rule that you will leave the office environment to eat your lunch, even if this means sitting in the park and eating it. Your surroundings are really important. The other important aspect is that you chew your food properly and are aware of the tastes and textures so that when you swallow, that food is ready to be digested.

While you are eating, be aware of every move you make. If you are eating from a plate, put your knife and fork down as you chew your food and pick them up when you are ready to take your next morsel of food. We tend to pile food into our systems, and this can result in more problems that can help to make your mental mood worse. Mindfulness eating means being aware of tastes and textures, aromas and every aspect of the act of eating and when you get into the habit of eating in this way, it will come naturally and even at business lunches, you will be able to put your knife and fork down on the plate between mouthfuls and thoroughly enjoy all the tastes and flavors of your food.

Exercise 4 - Mindfulness Touch and Taste Tests

You may wonder what the point of this exercise is, but the reason I want you to try it is that it helps you to develop your sense of taste and touch. How are these relevant to anger? The fact is that we have all forgotten to use these senses and are so busy focusing on what we see on the internet, on our phones, the TV, etc. that we don't take enough notice of the things around us. For the first test – which is touch – you may need to do this with your family members to see who is aware of what things are without even looking at them. You can use bags or even a pair of boots in which to hide objects that you have to touch and guess what they are. Items such as the grains of rice, or pasta, or anything dry can be used, and it's a fun exercise that your kids can join in with. As far as the taste test goes, this is slightly different in that you are given a taste of something blindfolded, and it's up to you to guess exactly what it is from the taste and the texture. As I said, these are simply fun tests, but among all of the seriousness of mindfulness, fun is okay too and may break the ice with people you have been previously angry with.

Exercise 5 – Mindfulness Anger Management Exercise

As you are seeking advice on anger management, it is assumed that you have admitted to yourself that you have an anger problem. This is an exercise that you can do when you feel that anger is about to happen. You will know because you will experience that rise in blood pressure, and the thought patterns that go through your head may not be as logical as you would like them to be. You have to get yourself out of the state of "fight or flight," which has been brought about by circumstances around you. The only way to do this is to remove yourself from the conversation and find a quiet place to sit down. If you can't do this for some reason, then do the exercise where you are, but distancing yourself from it will help to make it more effective.

Sit and close your eyes so that you are not disturbed by what's going on around you. Stop your thought processes and breathe. Count the inhale, count the exhale as I have shown you before, and as you do this, your mind will become calmer. If it doesn't happen straight away and you find thoughts flooding your head about what angered you, switch them off and go back to counting and breathing until you feel calm, take place within you. This is a great way to respond to anger because what you are doing is saying that the anger isn't justified, and you don't want it in your life. Anger can turn the whole world upside down. You don't necessarily see things from a great perspective when your thoughts are drowned by angry thoughts. Thus, calming your mind down allows you to gently address whatever it is that upset you with a calm state of mind. This calmness allows you to see the problem much clearer because you are letting go of those thoughts in order to clear your mind and are then approaching the problems with a clearer viewpoint.

Exercise 5 – Work and Undesirable Tasks

Choose a job that you don't particularly like doing but one that you know you should do. During the course of doing it, switch off all interruptions. No phone calls, no answering emails, no looking at alerts. Switch everything off. Approach the job with a mindful approach. In other words, be in the moment and do the job. Don't let anything at all stop you from achieving it. Be involved in it, and don't let your mind wander while you do it. Even something as seemingly simple as cleaning the kitchen floor can be enjoyable when you are mindful of the process. For example, watch how the colors change when you put wetness onto tiles. Watch how they shine. Enjoy the process and be absorbed by it, and you will not only get it done quicker, but you will actually get to enjoy doing it.

Exercise 6 – Empathy Exercise

To do this exercise, think of the last time that you lost your temper. Now, think from the perspective of the person you were angry with. How do they remember the situation? What did they feel like? What did your words do to them? You need to understand that everyone attacks life from one perspective, and it may not be the same as yours, but it doesn't make their perspective wrong. It just makes it different. When you are able to step into someone else's shoes occasionally, it helps you to learn empathy and to be a much calmer and empathetic person. Let me give you a demonstration using the example of my own anger – which is not expressed perhaps in the same way as yours. I have learned to control my anger over the course of years, but occasionally life throws a curveball, and I need to respond to angry thoughts. When my recent delivery arrived at the door, the box was broken, and I wanted to open it to check the contents before accepting it. The man at the door gave me the impression he didn't want to wait and made me feel a little angry because it's his job to wait and see if the parcel is acceptable. However, when I was a little friendlier in my tones, it turned out that the only reason he didn't want to wait was an urgent need to use the toilet. Having let him into my home for that purpose, once he had done, he was even happy to help me to unwrap every piece of the delivery to ensure that I was happy with it. In the past, I may have lost my temper, but approaching it from his angle and seeing that there may be a reason for his haste, I actually empathized, and he was willing to admit his needs. Often things are not what you suppose they are, and it's worthwhile stepping in and seeing it from another viewpoint.

Try these exercises to get you accustomed to using mindfulness and empathy because when you do, everything changes, and you have less to be angry about. It may be worthwhile coming back to this chapter after you have finished reading the book and randomly doing the exercises outlined here as part of your everyday life. Choose your moment – choose your exercise but remember that when you are doing mindful exercises of any kind, you need to be absorbed in the exercise and give it all your concentration. Let go of thoughts that are not relevant to the job.

How this helps you is that when you eventually learn mindful meditation, you will already know how to let go of thoughts, and that's half the battle. It's also half the battle when it comes to being in control of your anger. It's all part and parcel of the same thing. Some of these exercises have been fun ones and others more serious, but using them all to make use of your senses is a very sensible idea and will make you more aware of those senses, as you go through the process of introducing mindfulness into your life.

As a final exercise, listen to music and absorb it. It allows you to relax if you choose the right kind of music to lighten your mood. This can help you when you feel the weight of the world on your shoulders, and you may even find that it gives your mind a sufficient break from your anger for it to find solutions without even really trying.

Chapter Seven

Getting Back to the Basics

"Breath is the finest gift of nature.
Be grateful for this wonderful gift"

~ **Amit Ray**

I have worked with many people, from all walks of life, using mindfulness, and the beauty of this treatment for anger is that everyone responds positively to what happens within their bodies when they use mindfulness to help them to tackle anger management. For this chapter, I want to take you back to basics so that you understand the spiritual side of mindfulness. If you have time to go somewhere you recognize as a beauty spot at sunset or sunrise, then make those plans. Try to make the trip on your own; you need the silence of your mind to appreciate what I am about to demonstrate to you.

When you go to a place of beauty and nature, you find that it's overwhelmingly beautiful. If you are alone and the landscape around you is inspirational, it can make you feel very small. Why would you want to? Well, that's when spirituality begins. You appreciate all that is around you and use your senses to enjoy the moment. For example, breathe in the fresh air and try to describe what it tastes like. Try to close your eyes and feel the ambiance of that moment. Try to feel the cold or warm air on your skin. Try to listen to anything out there to listen to. For example, at the seashore, the sound of the birds or even the waves lapping in on the shore are a great distraction for a troubled mind. Now, open your eyes and see. Look at everything, and while you are looking, try not to think of anything in particular. Observe and use your sight to allow you the privilege of having this moment in this place. It's a wonderful feeling, and although people find this feeling in different scenarios, nature has a way of bringing it all together and making you feel overwhelmed at the beauty of the Earth.

Even if you can't go very far at all, you may even find stepping into your back yard to look at a rainbow can do the same thing. You use all of your senses to enjoy the moment, and it awakens something inside you called humility. Humility is going back to basics. It's that feeling that a child may feel the first time the child opens his/her eyes to look at something like light. There are no expectations. There are no disappointments. There is just the beauty of the world, and this wonder can fill your day with positivity. For example, one student explained to me about the cobwebs on the garden shrubs in the morning light, and how they resembled small diamonds. What you see when you really look at the world around you can be startlingly beautiful.

What Does This Have To Do With A Temper?

Well, if you allow yourself to use your senses in a situation such as this, you begin to see the bigger picture. That humility that you feel is a reminder that without judgment, you are able to look and see how small human beings are in the bigger picture, but that without all of those smaller pieces of the puzzle, the puzzle would never be complete.

At this moment, you feel no anger, no regret, no remorse, and nothing negative at all. Instead, you will find your heart filled with hope, love, and even optimism, and that helps to shield you from negative traits such as anger. Enjoy this moment and remember it because when you can see it in your mind's eye, you can use the scene that you are looking at to bring back positive vibes into your life; simply close your eyes and remember what you saw, instead of letting your mind be eroded by anger and angry thoughts. This is your peaceful haven, and it's something you can retain even when you are not able to visit this place. Remember the smells, the sights, the colors, the feelings, the emotions, and the touch against your skin.

What I want you to do now is to go home, and whenever you close your eyes, remember every part of that memory in detail. The beauty of the mind is that it can recall things that are specifically important to you. These are thoughts that recur. The hippocampus will remember things; all you are doing is reinforcing this positivity any time that you feel the need to, simply by sitting down, closing your eyes and being in that moment that you experienced. See it in all of its colors and shades, remember the smells, the sounds, the touch, the feel and everything about it that's good. People make the mistake of thinking that Buddhist temples are places of worship. They are not. They are places of inspiration and encourage those who go to them to use this inspiration to help them to be in the moment. At this moment, no one can hurt you. At this moment, you can enjoy everything about that place that brought you back to a state of humility. There is nothing more spiritual than experiencing this inner depth and beauty, and everyone has the potential to use it to better themselves. This is your opportunity. Take it to help you over the hurdles of the future and remember it as often as possible, so that your mind knows the place you seek when you need it as a refuge from the world.

The spiritual side of mindfulness belongs to everyone, regardless of their religious affiliation. You don't even have to be a believer to believe in what you see with your own eyes that surpasses the normal scene you may see every day. When you find the place that does this to you, you have found a magical place that can help you through many of the problems you are going to encounter during your life. There is a special place that I use for this purpose when I feel at odds with the world, and it is on top of a hill, with a 360 degrees view of the countryside with hills and trees, fields and farms, and wildlife everywhere. I love to use this place at sunset or sunrise to remind me of the beauty of the world that I live in and the small size of the problems that I am encountering.

When you do that, it kind of puts things into perspective, and although that place was a refuge for me as a child, it still holds the same fascination, and when you find your special place, it will be the same.

Sometimes we need to see the bigger picture to realize the smallness of our own dilemmas, and it helps to put a lot of things into perspective. When Alan found out that his son was gay, his anger was his only refuge at the time, which alienated his son from him and created problems with his wife. However, his real refuge was found in the stars at night, and when he took himself off to his vantage point of preference, he realized how small-minded he had been and upon coming home, was able to telephone his son and put things right. The small problems that we face every day of our lives are but hiccups along the road of life. They are tiny specks on the horizon, and the spiritual self will recognize them as such and help you to overcome them. Anger doesn't solve anything. Understanding and empathy does. By talking things through with his son, he was able to see that his son's life made the boy happy, and that was more important than personal restrictions and biases. It often is, and anger does nothing to overcome these hurdles and tends to make greater divisions between people instead of creating bridges by which those individuals can understand each other.

Chapter Eight

Using a Body Scan

You may never have heard of a body scan, but this is a very useful tool for those who are learning mindfulness. It helps to relax the body and would be a good exercise to try at bedtime or in the late afternoon when you are alone, and you want to relax for a short while. The bedroom is where this exercise takes place, and you need to be dressed comfortably so that nothing is tight, such as your waistband or your necktie. In fact, it's better in pajamas than in restrictive clothing. The problem with the clothing that we tend to wear is that it's sometimes a distraction, and that's what we are trying to get rid of for this exercise.

You may be accustomed to using two pillows, but for this exercise, I want you to use one so that your breathing is optimal, and your windpipe is in a better position to breathe without obstruction. Lie on your back on the bed and place your hands by your sides. Start to breathe in to a count of eight and out to a count of ten until you feel that you are breathing to a rhythm. Keep on inhaling through the nostrils and breathing out. When you do achieve that rhythm, close your eyes and make sure that there are no distractions in the room that can take your attention away from the body scan.

Now concentrate on your toes. Think of your big toes first and feel them. Tense them up and then relax them and feel how heavy they feel as they relax on the bed. The next thing to think of is your other toes. Continue to breathe in the same way and think of the other toes and tense them up. Then relax them and feel them relax before moving on up the body through the different areas of the body such as the ankles, the calf, the knee, the thigh, the hips, the waist, the chest, the fingers, the hands, the forearm, and upper arm and do the same thing – tensing that part of your body and then relaxing it. While you are doing this, keep the breathing regular so that your heartbeat slows, and your blood pressure goes down. This is one of the most relaxing exercises that you can do, but you need to keep your mind occupied with the breathing and the parts of the body, and if your mind wanders, you pull it back to this moment and go back to the toes again to start the scan afresh.

By the end of the session, you will feel very relaxed, and the reason I am teaching you to do this is because it helps you with the mindfulness exercises later in the book and it also gives you instant release from anxiety so that the exercise can be used to help you to resolve anger issues that are ongoing. You will find that breathing, in conjunction with the sensitivity to your body parts, will relax you, and that's very helpful indeed. It puts distance between you and the object of your anger so that you are able to look at your problems from a more neutral stance, once you are relaxed and thinking clearly.

Body scans can be done in an ambiance of semi-darkness if this helps you, and by drawing the drapes in your bedroom, you are taking away more distractions than necessary, and the ambiance can be very relaxing indeed. However, be aware that you will experience a drop-in blood pressure and heart rate, so when you have finished, it's not a good idea to get up too quickly. Thus, you should put aside about half an hour for this exercise and then take your time to dress and go back to your normal everyday life. If you find that music relaxes you, you can also use this as a background, but the music should not be loud. It is simply to hush the mind so that you can concentrate on the body scan in a more effective way. When you are angry, this helps because it causes the right kind of distraction and helps you to keep your breathing in rhythm.

As you get more into the mindfulness experience, you may even find that you create an area for yourself where you can meditate; a place where you have inspirational things around you to help you relax. This may be a good area to lie down on a yoga mat and do the body scan instead of using your bed. However, do make sure that your clothing is comfortable and that your head is supported by a good pillow. Your posture really matters because whether you know it or not, everyone has energy points throughout their bodies, and the energy cannot reach them if you are hunched up or in an uncomfortable position. Even if you tend to lie on your side to sleep, don't use this position for the scan.

If you have problems sleeping, you can also use this to get the anger out of your mind at the end of the day so that you get better quality sleep. In the next chapter, we are going to be touching on why mindfulness meditation works and what it's doing to your approach to life. It's quite important that you understand the process so that you can make the most of the experience without being left with all kinds of questions about the use of mindfulness meditation and its benefits. You can also use a body scan sitting up if you find that your anger levels are rising. Simply put the anger out of your mind and start by thinking of your feet and working through the different parts of your body to relax them. Of course, it won't send you to sleep if you are sitting up, but what it will do is take your mind off what it was that was making you angry in the first place.

Chapter Nine

The Benefits of Mindfulness Meditation

Some people who suffer from anger can't slow themselves down and worry about whether meditation will work for them. The fact is that it works for anyone who makes this a regular part of their day. The reason why you are expected to meditate every day is so you can create a habit that is helpful to you when dealing with your anger problem. How does it do that? When you are angry, it's because you are reacting to something that has made you angry. Does everyone react in a negative manner? Of course not, but that's because anger starts in mind, and everyone's mind is different. Some people never get angry. They are able to look at a problem from various perspectives and come up with answers. Others get confusing messages, and because of their frustration, they tend to react in an angry manner. It's because of something that the Buddhists refer to as the "monkey mind" or the mind that is allowed to carry on doing what it does with no real measure of control. In the same way, some people react to pain in different ways or to different events in life as this kind of reaction isn't just confined to people who have anger issues.

The benefits of mindfulness include the following:

- It helps to lower your blood pressure

- It slows your heart down
- It helps you to empty the "monkey mind."
- It helps you to put thoughts in order
- It clears the mind
- It cuts down stress
- It allows you to see the world in a different manner
- It helps you to be more compassionate

And that's just the start. Mindfulness meditation helps you to take judgment out of the question. If you don't judge others, you tend to be more tolerant and understanding of the fact that everyone approaches things in a different manner. Your child didn't do something wrong to upset you. He did it because he is a child experimenting with life and learning about his own limitations. Stop seeing things that happen in your life as being purposeful acts to make you angry. No one can make you angry. It is your own mind that creates anger, and if mindfulness helps you to see life in this manner, rather than in a judgmental manner, your anger problems will diminish. Anger tends to be based on the bias of some kind, and mindfulness helps to break the barriers and makes you less closed-minded. You are more empathetic and can see problems in life from a clearer standpoint. That means that you are not so often overwhelmed by life and can get through more work in less time.

Other benefits of mindfulness are that you are not likely to succumb to mental problems that may cause anxiety. Anxiety is a little like a diving board for anger. The anxiety triggers all of the hormones in your body to be released, and when they are, they irritate the system sufficiently so that you have to release that anger. It's normal, and it's a natural response to this overwhelming feeling of hopelessness. However, mindfulness meditation, once a day for 20 minutes, can take away that response and train your mind to be more positively influenced by the world around you.

I asked many students who start mindfulness, whether it made a difference in their lives, and the results were always the same. It did make a difference, and even if a session was missed from time to time, the benefits far outweighed the inconvenience. People felt smarter. They felt empowered, and they felt positive, which are feelings that anger robs us of. Let's look at a typical scenario.

Your Partner Does Something That Really Bugs You

There was no intention on their part to hurt you, but you were surprised by their action, and it sent your whole system into this natural overload, questioning their motives and being angry about what they did. What this shows is that you don't actually take the time to talk with your partner. Otherwise, you may have been less surprised by their actions and more compassionate toward their needs. When you practice mindfulness, you spend more time present in your life, rather than letting your mind wander to past things or to worry about things that haven't happened yet, so you are much more likely to understand your partner's point of view. You listen more and have more space in your mind to find solutions to your problems and to the problems of your partner.

So Why Do People Get Angry?

People who are angry can feel that way because of circumstances or because they feel that they have no control over a situation. For example, a man who cannot earn sufficient to keep his family may see this lack of "manhood" as a threat to who he is. In fact, a man can be equally helpful in the home and live a perfectly happy existence as a house husband if he views his role as being sufficiently important to the happiness of the family. In a man who views it in this way, there would be no anger, because his work is still something he sees as valuable. The angry man, however, sees that his lack of contribution makes him less of a man. He then gets angry with his partner and misplaces his anger because he doesn't know how to cope with his situation in any other way.

In all of the scenarios that I have described, mindfulness helps you to overcome the anxiety that leads to anger, and thus anger doesn't happen. You learn compassion, you learn to forgive, you learn to move on, and you also learn how to forgive yourself for your shortcomings and learn to appreciate who you are and the role that you play in life. Mindfulness teaches you that you can be flexible and that you don't have to conform to other people's standards. It teaches you that every single moment in our lives is different, and thus, what we are angry about at this moment may not necessarily anger us in the future, and thus it isn't worth expending the energy needed to get angry. It is far better to address the problem in a more constructive way.

The biggest benefit of mindfulness is that it will help the following:

- Your communication skills with others
- Your acceptance of situations beyond your control
- Your ability to think things through
- Your learning ability

You open yourself up to a new experience, and when you do that, you often find that the person you thought had been drowned out by anger or anxiety is still there, intact, but you need to empty out the clutter to find him/her. Decluttering the mind is something that's quite fashionable at the moment for a very good reason. We, as human beings, fill out minds with stimuli from all directions, and there's no wonder that people get confused and angry or even socially anxious.

The mind cannot cope with life, and anger is simply letting that extra energy out that shows your frustration. What if I told you mindfulness could help you to do the same thing? It can, and you never need to get angry again. Your mind will find a new way to cope with the bad things that happen in life, and you will become more philosophical rather than reactional in your responses, finding answers calmly instead of having to expend negative energy on anger.

Chapter Ten

Count and Breathe

You have already learned to breathe in a certain way through the chapters of this book, but this particular chapter is an exercise in using mindfulness and breathing to get you over a very angry phase. As you already know, what happens in the body when you lose your temper is:

- Your blood pressure rises

- Your heartbeat goes up

- Your testosterone levels rise

- Cortisol release into the body is slowed down

Brain activity changes too, and this can be stopped in its tracks by mindfulness. What's happening in your body is that your stress levels are less in control because you need cortisol to help control this. This of your confusion and anger as being a chemical reaction, and you wouldn't be too far off the truth. The fact is that stress of any kind can trigger all kinds of activity in the body that you are totally unaware of. The hippocampus is also taking notice of what's happening to you and what provoked it; that's unfortunate because, if it sees you reacting with anger to a set of circumstances, when those circumstances happen again the hippocampus will tell all of the different parts of your brain that anger is your normal response. That is what we need to change.

You may not think that you can change these memories stored in the hippocampus, but you can. When you create new habits they are stored in the hippocampus. The new habits replace old habits, ensuring that there is always a way to change things by changing what's stored in the hippocampus. It isn't about changing who you are and how you react at this present moment, but about changing your reactions, so the brain records something entirely more suitable than anger. So, you already know what makes you angry, but you have to educate yourself on how to redirect that so that it's a more acceptable kind of response than anger. Mindfulness helps you to do this.

Whether you know it or not, the way you breathe affects the workings of your body. If you breathe in too much oxygen, you are likely to over-oxygenate and this can cause you to become even hotter under the collar, causing you anxiety and perhaps even depression. However, when you regulate the amount of oxygen going into your body, you help it to remain calm. The breathing exercises shown here are to help your body to do this and should be employed if you find yourself building up to anger. From the moment that you feel your mind change in pace because something has angered you, I want you to start breathing through the nostrils and be aware of the breath as you count to eight and then breathe out to the count of ten. If you are in a position where you cannot get away from the source of your anger, bring your mind into this moment and let go of the thoughts of anger. You can deal with these later when you are calm. For the time being, breathe in and out in this way, and don't show your anger. You are trying to change the reaction from anger to calm because that's what you want the hippocampus to record as your response to stress. Think about what color the sky is; look at everything that is touched by your senses and feel it with every sense that you have.

Focused Breathing Exercise

This is another breathing exercise that you can use when you feel that you need clarity of thought and don't want anger to be the result of whatever is happening around you. Focused breathing helps you to empty your mind of the things that you really don't want there and also help you to be able to think clearly after an event has happened that makes you angry. In this case, it doesn't matter whether you have the ability to draw. Even a child can use this to stop tantrums from happening, so you don't have the excuse that you have no drawing talent.

I want you to sit in a place where you are comfortable and make sure that your back is straight. It's easy to do at work because many of the office seats are hard and tend to be made so that they give you back the correct support. The only thing is that you do need to be away from noise and confusion to do this exercise. I have even known people who use the lady's room or the men's cloakroom to do it. When you are seated, place your hands in your lap and close your eyes. Your feet should be flat on the floor. Now, I want you to draw an image of a house in your mind. It can be as complex or as simple as you like, but I want you to use your mind's eye to see the colors and see the lines that make up the drawing of the outline, the windows, the roof, the door, and every part of that house. While you are drawing, breathe in through the nostrils as I have shown you before to the count of seven and then breathe out to the count of ten and keep this breathing rhythm going while you draw your house. Add the garden, and focus on creating that house and garden, without letting the angry thoughts come back to you during the whole exercise. When you are happy that you have finished the drawing, open your eyes, and bring your breathing back to normal slowly. Do not get up straight away but let your body come back to your normal relaxed state.

This exercise does not avoid anger. What it does is take your mind away from the anger and redirect it toward something very creative, using that part of the brain that deals with creativity. When you do this, you are able to let go of anger, and when you are calm, you will be able to find better solutions than anger to deal with whatever it is that made you angry in the first place.

Expelling Anger Through The Breathing

This is yet another method that you can use to dispel anger. Breathe in through the nostrils to the count of eight and then breathe out as a snort as if you are trying to blow all of the bad stuff out of your system. You may be looked at strangely if you try doing this in a place where people can see you, so choose somewhere where you can be alone while you use this method. Breathe in – and then imagine you are a dragon getting rid of all that fire inside you on the outward breath. Breathe in and do the same again until you get to the stage where the anger has diminished.

The 4-7-8 Method of Breathing

This was a method devised by Dr. Andrew Weil, and I have tested this on people who suffer from anger, and it is effective. For this exercise to work, you need to be sitting straight with your feet flat on the floor. Breathe into the count of four, hold the breath for the count of seven and breathe out to the count of eight. You are getting rid of excess in your bloodstream by breathing in this way, and this excess consists of oxygen, which has been built up through erratic breathing while experiencing anxiety or tenseness that usually leads to anger. Try it several times a day if you want to since no one will know you are doing it as it's not an obvious breathing exercise at all, but does help to regulate the amount of oxygen which can excite you and make you feel edgy. When you get rid of that excess, you are naturally calmer.

Alternate Nostril Breathing

When anger wears you down, and you feel apathy setting in, this exercise can help to re-energize you but only use it when you want that energy rather than using this when you have excess energy. Hold your thumb over your right nostril and breathe in through the left nostril. Let go of the right nostril and breathe out. The idea is that you use alternate nostrils for breathing in and out over a period of about five minutes. While you are doing this, concentrate on what you are doing rather than the thoughts that have driven you to this apathy in the first place.

We have covered much that includes breathing, but this is the mainstay for mindfulness meditation, and it is better that you are aware of the method before you try to meditate. Meditation is not complex, but people make it complex by mentally arguing with the process. In the case of Elizabeth Gilbert, in the book Eat, Pray, Love, what she was fighting was the process of letting go of thoughts, as she thought that these are an important part of who she was although once she learned the method, she suddenly discovered that the only thing holding her back in her life was indeed her thought processes and once she was able to change them, she was also able to change the way that she lived her life. You can do the same, once you understand the significance of silence in mind and see how it can help you.

In the next chapters, we are going to look at mindfulness meditation and prepare you for this journey into a new you. You may not feel that you want to be anything different from who you are now, but it isn't exactly you that changes. What changes is the way that your mind processes thoughts.

Please do not skip reading the preliminary parts of learning about meditation because these are necessary to help you to succeed. Although they may have little significance at the moment, they will in due course, and an understanding of how your brain works helps you to make it work more effectively and rid yourself of the anger that you feel about life. Once you are rid of the anger, things improve enormously, and you start to feel much happier.

Chapter Eleven

Preparing Yourself for Daily Meditation

I explained in an earlier chapter how the hippocampus works at recording all of the events in your life that seem to be significant to you. How does it know what's significant? It knows because it sees and recognizes behavior patterns. For example, if you are afraid of spiders, it will know your obvious response to seeing a spider and will act quicker than the conscious mind will to remind you that there is a spider present. It's the body's way of protecting you, but it's also a little mischievous when it comes to predicting how you will behave. For example, if a person makes you angry, your hippocampus knows about it, and when that person is near, you will be on alert because of this prior knowledge. Habits form during the course of your lifetime, and these habits are recorded inside your hippocampus, which tells you it's time for a cigarette or that you need coffee, or indeed that you need to urinate. Your body creates patterns, and of course, the hippocampus jumps in and makes you react to whatever is happening in your life.

What Does This Have To Do With Meditation?

Well, the fact of the matter is that if you make meditation a daily habit, after about a month, you won't even have to make an effort to do it. It will be something you do without even thinking about it because it's recognized as a habit. The idea of making meditation a daily event is so that it reinforces certain values into your mind and relaxes you and enables you to deal with situations without letting the "monkey mind" get in the way of making decisions without getting angry. The monkey mind is the mind that is filled with thoughts or half-opened cardboard boxes of emotions that are unsettled. This is what gets in the way of clear thought. If you mess up at work, the chances are that the monkey mind took your attention off work. If you mess up in a relationship, it's probably because your mind was too busy with other things to remember that it was your anniversary or something rather important. The whole point is that your mind is too chock full of thoughts for clarity, and meditation helps to put the mind into a state where you can see solutions clearly and don't have problems processing information.

Committing to Meditation

It's a good idea to arrange a place for your daily meditation. It may be in your bedroom, or it could be in a quiet room in your house or even in your garden or yard. The point is that this area should allow you to sit in silence and not be too distracted by what's going on around you. You can make it more inspirational by adding things that do inspire you, such as a picture, candles, or even a Buddha statue. Remember that Buddha isn't a God at all. He is an inspiration, and if it works for you, then go for it. If you think that you will sit on the floor, you may need to get yourself a yoga mat and a cushion so that you can hold the necessary stance for your meditation. The cushion should be hard enough to support your body without getting uncomfortable.

You also need to choose clothing in which to meditate, and these should be clothes that do not distract you. Things that could distract you are the following:

- A tight neckline
- A tight waistband
- Uncomfortable shoes
- Clothing that makes you itch

The whole point of choosing something loose is so that the clothing is not in your thoughts when you meditate. You have energy centers all through your body and may have to practice the seating position a couple of times until you are happy with it. If you are in any way handicapped and cannot sit on a cushion on the floor, don't worry. You can also meditate while sitting on a straight-backed chair, but do not lean back because your spine should be straight during the whole process of meditation.

Seating Position

Practice this now so that when you choose to meditate, you are ready and able to meditate without having to give the position much thought. You should place yourself onto your cushion and make sure that your back is straight. Bend your knees and make sure that your ankles are crossed. There is no need at all to take up the full lotus position because you are not experienced at this, and it may make you too uncomfortable when you first start. Your arms should be bent at the elbows, and your hands should be cupped in an upward direction with one hand resting on the other. If you are right-handed, let the right hand support the left. If you are left-handed, let the left hand support the other. Touch your thumbs together.

If you are using a chair for meditation, the stance is slightly different. In this case, sit with your feet flat on the floor with your back straight at all times, and your head slightly lowered to open up your breathing and make it easier. Rest your hands on your lap, this time with the hands cupped together and turned up toward the ceiling.

Mindfulness And The Environment You Meditate In

Close your eyes for a moment and try to imagine that you are about to meditate. Use all of your senses to find out how the area you have chosen for your meditation feels. What can you hear? What can you smell? What can you taste? What can you feel? If you feel drafts, then you need to eliminate these before you meditate. If you are interrupted by noise, is there any way that you can choose a time when those noises won't be apparent. The ideal time to meditate daily will be either first thing in the morning or before your dinner in the evening.

It's important to understand that meditation takes consistency and that the time that you choose should be a regular time each day. If you miss a day, you can, of course, compensate for that by simply being mindful during the day, but it's a good habit to get into on a regular basis because the more you get into meditation, the better you feel and the more capable you feel of handling your anger.

When Should You Meditate?

It is not a good idea to meditate after eating because your digestive system is working and will remind you of that fact while you meditate. Give your body time to digest food before you meditate and try to meditate either before a meal or at least two hours after eating so that your food is digested. It's also not a good time to meditate when your mind is hyped up, so try to avoid it after watching an action movie, or after having been angry at traffic for the past hour or so. The ideal times tend to be first thing in the morning or, as stated above, before your evening meal. If you can get members of your family to understand that you need this time alone, this is helpful.

The very best time to meditate is always going to be when you feel calm and unhurried. It will only take you about half an hour at the most when you begin. You may find that you want to meditate for a longer period once you have started, but that's your choice. If you set your alarm clock half an hour earlier, this means that you won't be any later for work and will be able to meditate before the rest of your household has arisen.

Chapter Twelve

Mindful Meditation in Practice

When you set yourself up for Mindfulness meditation, it's a good idea to have a clock within sight so that you don't overrun your time and make yourself late for work. You will eventually get to know exactly how long your sessions are, but for the time being, it will be difficult to gauge. Sit down in your chosen position. If you choose to use a chair, take the following stance:

Sit on the chair with your back straight and your feet flat on the floor.

Place one hand in the other with the palms upward and touch thumbs.

If you choose to use a yoga mat and a cushion, then this is the position that you need to be in before you place your hands cupped in front of you. Notice how the legs are bent at the knees, and the ankles are crossed.

You don't need to make it any more complex than this. The cushion that you use should give you adequate support. Now cup your hands together and touch your thumbs together. The idea is that you now sway from left to right to make sure that you are comfortable. Remember that even five minutes in a position that is uncomfortable for the body can be too much. When you find your center by swaying from left to right, you stand a better chance of staying comfortable during the process of meditation.

Note the time and then close your eyes. Start to breathe and to count as you inhale through the nostrils count to eight and feel the air going right down into your upper abdomen. Then breathe out to the count of ten. Do this over and over again until you are happy with the rhythm of your breathing. Try to avoid thinking of anything at all except the counting and breathing, and when you know that the rhythm is right, count one, at the end of the inhale and exhale, then two at the end of the inhale and exhale, and so on until you reach ten.

If thoughts come into your mind, you must learn to dismiss them as not being valid to this moment in time. If they do invade, you simply go back to one again and start again. All the time that you are breathing and thinking only of the breath, you are allowing your mind to feel free from all of the thoughts and worries of the world; you are staying in the same place, in this very moment, breathing in and out and being aware of the way that your body feels as you do so. As long as you keep your thoughts at this moment, then they are allowed. For example, if you think that you would like to try inspired meditation, then why not light a candle, and instead of closing your eyes, concentrate on the flame of the candle as you breathe in and out and count the breaths. Do not use anything that may distract you from the act of meditation. I always tell beginners to meditate with their eyes closed because it helps to stop distractions. You may not know it, but your eyes can very easily be pulled to the right or the left simply by noticing a movement, and that distracts the whole process. Thus, for the time being, keeping your eyes closed helps you to concentrate on the breath and the moment.

If you need to imagine the breath like a flame going inside you and then being exhaled, that's okay; your thought is centered upon the breath. However, avoid thoughts that form chains of logic in your mind, because meditation is a time just to be, rather than think about being. Don't beat yourself up if thoughts creep in. They will at first because you think so many thoughts a day that it's going to be hard to switch them off at first. Simply acknowledge the thought and then let go of it.

You may be wondering what the point of the exercise is, as many students ask me questions about meditation, and I will try to answer common ones in this section:

Why Do You Need To Be Aware Of The Breath?

Because the breath is happening now, and you are trying to center yourself upon this moment. The breath is regular and easy to center your mind upon without having to go into the realms of deep thought. If you have to concentrate, you can't meditate, so just let go and be in the breath.

What Can I Do If Thoughts Won't Stop?

You are in control of your thought processes. However, because of habit, it will take a while before you are able to let go of thoughts, and you can practice this by recognizing the things that you do almost as second nature. For example, when you get up in the morning, you are not consciously aware of how you get out of bed. You simply do it. You probably don't think about cleaning your teeth; you just do it. You probably don't give a second thought about going to the toilet –

you just do it. When you get used to doing meditation, all of the automated actions become second nature; you won't have to think about it, you will just do it. The importance of doing it daily applies here because you are trying to form a new habit – one that will help you manage your anger. If thoughts don't stop, simply use your concentration to think about your breath, so that the thoughts can't form chains. At first, it will be a conscious decision, but when you get accustomed to meditation, you don't need to think about it anymore.

What If My Sitting Position Is Uncomfortable?

Well, here you won't have taken enough time getting yourself comfortable in the first place, which is why swaying is important. Although you may not think that 15 minutes of sitting in the same position can hurt, if you haven't balanced yourself out, it can. People in strict meditation routines won't move because they are uncomfortable, but will learn from it to position themselves correctly the next time.

What If I Get Interrupted While I Am Meditating?

It's best that you don't get interrupted, and to avoid this, try to put a notice on the door "Do not disturb" or let family members know that when you are meditating, you need to be alone and uninterrupted. If you are interrupted, don't get up too quickly as your heartbeat will be slower, and your blood pressure will have gone down. Simply answer from where you are and continue to meditate.

Can I Meditate With Others?

You can, but it's pretty hard to arrange a daily meditation routine when you are depending on others being there. For your daily meditation, it is, therefore, better that you meditate alone. If you find that opportunity presents itself to go to a meditation center or a yoga class, then treat that differently and by all means go because the more input you get on the process of meditation, the better.

Can I Meditate After Breakfast?

It's best that you never meditate after eating because your stomach will remind you that it is working. Digestion takes a lot of energy away from the process of meditating, so this is not the ideal time to meditate. By all means, eat your breakfast after your meditation session but never before.

What Does It Mean To Let Go Of Thoughts?

Many of the thoughts that we have during the day are vague. They may relate to events that have happened in the past, or they may relate to things that are going to happen. During meditation, you need to be centered at the moment, so thinking about the past won't help you, and thinking about the future takes you out of the moment. We waste a lot of our lives thinking about things that don't even matter anymore – particularly when we have anger issues. In the next chapter, I am going to go into specifics of letting go, but for the time being, if you are in the moment and not thinking about past or present, then you have let go of your thoughts.

Try this exercise for a moment. Sit in a chair and breathe in and out and close your eyes to the world. Now try to stop thinking. It's not the easiest thing in the world to do. Now, when a thought happens, ask yourself if it's relevant to this moment, and if it is not, let it go. You will find this to be the most difficult lesson of all, especially if you have an anger problem because people who are angry tend to hold onto things for a longer period of time than they need to. They are trying to find solutions, but by trying in this way, they complicate matters even further, whereas meditation and a mind clear of thought will help them to find logical conclusions to their problems without all of the mind work.

Focused Meditation

If you find that you can't do mindfulness meditation, you can use another type of meditation that is equally mindful; this type focuses the mind on something specific so you don't have a void like you do when you close your eyes. In this case, the process is exactly the same, but you need to choose something upon which to focus while you do the breathing that takes you into meditation. A candle may do the trick, or you may want to have a photo of someone important to you to remind you of why you want to work on your anger-management in the first place. Meditate as you would otherwise, but keep your eyes on the focal point of your meditation, which may help you to stop thoughts from entering your mind while you are trying to empty the mind of thoughts.

Chapter Thirteen

Letting Go Of Thoughts

Here are some exercises that will help you to let go of thoughts. Think of a thought as an invader of your private space and choose a piece of music that you can get totally absorbed in. Quite often, the noise of life goes on, and we take very little notice of it going on in our heads, but this exercise will help you to understand the extent of your problem. Lie down and listen to that piece of music and every time a thought arises that has nothing to do with the music, switch off the thought and discipline yourself to go back to being absorbed by the music. It's good training and if you need a headset to do this, by all means, use one. You don't need the music so loud that it energizes you. You need music that requires listening to, and the choice should be something that relaxes you.

In a situation like this, it's very easy to let go of thoughts because you have something else to concentrate your mind on. However, in life in general, we don't have that, so we bottle up all the thoughts until they overwhelm us. Instead of doing that, let's look at the different types of thoughts that may happen during the course of even half an hour:

- Negative self-image thoughts

- Negative thoughts about a situation or person
- Thoughts evoked by emotions
- Thoughts about things you have to do
- Thoughts about things you haven't done
- Abstract thoughts that appeared to come from nowhere

Your thoughts need to be trained. It's only a thought, and until it is acted on, it has no value to you at all. If the thoughts are negative and you don't resolve them, they can add to your negativity, so you need to decide:

- Which thoughts need my immediate attention?
- Which thoughts are irrelevant at this moment in time?
- Which thoughts are making me negative?

Then look at the problems of your life. There are some things that you can do absolutely nothing about. You were born too short. You are too plump. Your hair won't grow. Your nose is too big. Thoughts about things that you cannot change are totally wasted thoughts and take up space in your mind that only adds negativity to your day. These are thoughts you can banish at a moment's notice because they feed your anger and your negativity. To banish these thoughts, reframe them and answer them with something more positive and then let go. For example, "I am too short" can be replaced by "My stature in life cannot be measured by my height." There are always counter-arguments to negative comments in your head that serve no positive purpose. These are the most important thoughts to let go of because you can't do anything about them, and going over them time and again simply adds to your dissatisfaction with life. Imagine them like balloons, and when you recognize one of these thoughts coming to your mind, pop it.

Emotional Thoughts

Emotional thoughts are not always logical, and often people who get angry easily are going to have emotional thoughts. They think with their emotions rather than using logic to conclude problems that happen in their lives. There is a very good way to banish the emotional thoughts of a negative manner by using mindfulness. When you know that you are surrounded by negativity and your thoughts are edging you toward anger, the best thing to do is to take those thoughts, focus on them briefly, and then banish them. For example, you know that people around you are doing things that you don't particularly like, but you also know that the disciplinarian you have inside isn't working too well. Instead of trying to account for the actions of others, use affirmations to be more accountable for what's going on in your mind. That doesn't mean sitting in front of a mirror and telling yourself you are beautiful. I have read this advice all over the Internet, and it's not very encouraging for people who know that they aren't that beautiful. Instead of using affirmations that don't convince anyone, look around you and divert your thoughts to things around you that form part of this moment.

There's a very good saying by the Dalai Lama, which is useful in this instance because it shows you how much people waste their lives in the land of thoughts. When he was asked what surprised him the most about mankind, this was his answer:

"Man! Because he sacrifices his health in order to make money. Then he sacrifices money to recuperate his health. And then he is so anxious about the future that he does not enjoy the present; the result being that he does not live in the present or the future; he lives as if he is never going to die, and then dies having never really lived."

These are words worth remembering when you find that emotional thoughts are taking over. Just be in the moment for a minute rather than allowing emotions to take over, and focus on what all of your senses are feeling at this moment in time.

- The sense of taste
- The sense of touch
- The sense of hearing
- The sense of sight
- The sense of intuition

And use these thoughts to replace the negative thoughts or the thoughts that revolve around emotions. These are very helpful senses to use when you make affirmations because you can make affirmations that really are true. For example:

- The coffee I am drinking is absolutely delicious

- The perfume that woman is wearing is wonderful

- I can see that there is not a cloud in the sky

- I am so lucky to be able to see the colors and the sights of the city

- I feel very honored to have all my senses

In other words, step into the moment and start to tell yourself what's good about this moment in time. I remember standing at the graveside of a loved one when they were being buried, and emotional thoughts took over – not the sort that makes you angry, but the sort that provokes negative emotions none the less. Then I started to look around me at nature and was astounded that, as my friend had died, a primrose had peeked its head out of the winter hedgerow and was bringing a small speck of beauty to the world. When faced with a situation that may have angered me in the past, I tend to look toward nature rather a lot to enjoy the moment in time, and these positive statements that you make instead of expanding the negativity help you to keep your emotions in control. Thus, anger doesn't have to happen.

Another thing that tends to bring negative thoughts to a standstill is surrounding yourself with people who are positive. If you find that you are always surrounded by negative people, it's very easy to let that negativity take over. There must be some people in your life who tire you mentally. These are the people to make less contact with because they are the type of people who drain you. However, people who are happy and who are positive are much more likely to make you feel positive and get rid of those angry thoughts.

As another way to get rid of thoughts, I want you to close your eyes for a moment and remember the most glorious day of your life. It may have been when you were a child. It may have been when you first fell in love or when you received recognition for something that you did. As you close your eyes, I want you to see the situation in full color and the people you were with and experience those emotions again. This is the only time that is thinking about the past is useful to you. When you find yourself out of control and angry, keep this thought as your escape route; simply close off your mind to what's making you angry and replace it with your own little bit of paradise. Accompany it with deep breathing so that when you have to face the situation that made you angry, you are calmer and more capable of coming up with solutions that don't cause anger.

An Exercise in Mind Shifting

I don't suggest that you do this every day. However, for the sake of showing you how temporary the thought process is, I want you to think of the worst thing that ever happened to you. Feel the emotions, feel the hurt, and then switch over to that happiest day as quickly as you can so that you are overtaken by happier thoughts. You use the same methods when you have things happening in your life that you want to shift out of your mind. Breathe deeply, think of what it is that's bothering you and tell it that it isn't appropriate at this time, and then let go, shifting your mind over to what's happening in the real here and now that is positive.

Mind shifting teaches you to be mindful. What mindfulness means is being aware of your thoughts and being in control of this moment. If thoughts come that are not relevant to this moment, let them go and think thoughts that are. Often people can't go to sleep because they become acutely aware that they cannot go to sleep, and instead of relaxing into sleep, the thoughts of their inability to sleep take over, and they can't sleep. If they let go of the idea that they cannot sleep and simply start thinking in terms of relaxation and slumber, the chances are that they will sleep better than they remember sleeping before because the thoughts shape what happens on the outside. Angry thoughts do the same thing. They make you appear ugly to others. People are intimidated by anger and will resist being nice to someone who appears to be angry. Anger causes fear. Reflective thought and help don't. You have to know which thoughts are appropriate at which given time, and that's merely a matter of practice. When you respond to life with positivity and are at the moment, you are less stressed. You are also much calmer, and you will find that mindfulness allows you to drop thoughts whenever and wherever you want to, and move to thoughts that are more productive or that feed you positivity instead of negativity.

The mindfulness meditation that you do each day empties out the mind, so it's receptive to what's happening in the day. Your mind no longer clogged by thoughts of the past, and you don't act in a worried manner. Worry serves no purpose. Use a diary system to remember important things, and then once it's written down, you don't have to worry about it anymore. Don't keep storing stuff in your head that can be lightened by letting go of thoughts. Many people who suffer from anger management problems feel bad about who they are. Perhaps they had a bad experience and feel guilty about it, or feel that they are treading on eggshells when they are with certain people. Instead of letting those eggshells make you walk carefully, watch them hatch into beautiful creatures and let whatever is supposed to happen simply happen.

Chapter Fourteen

Letting go of Judgment and Blame

This is one of the hardest aspects of mindfulness for people to grasp. When you judge yourself or others, you are setting up hurdles. These people may not match your expectations, or you may be angry because you don't meet your own expectations, but what if those expectations were not there in the first place? The fact is that every human being is entitled to their own approach to life, and just because someone disagrees with you doesn't make them wrong and you right. You have to learn empathy because this helps you to take judgment out of the picture.

So How Do You Let Go of Judgment?

Think about all of your friends for a moment and write down their names. Then as you read them, one at a time, try to view this situation from their perspective.

I cannot go any further. My legs are too tired and my hands too cold.

Point to the friend's name and close your eyes and think about how that person would respond to that situation. Be that person. Imagine being in their shoes because each human being will approach life situations from different angles, and you can't know what empathy is until you have been there. As you work your way through your list of friends and imagine being that person in that situation, you will see something that is surprisingly obvious. That is that different people have different perspectives. What is happening in each case scenario is exactly the same, but because a person is different, they see things differently. Let me show you this with a number of my friends, whose names I have changed intentionally as this isn't personal at all.

Mary – determined and strong, regardless of how she feels, will drag her legs forward and even find encouragement for people around her, regardless of her own discomfort.

Susan – Susan will go slowly and will probably complain because it's her way of coping, and it helps her to balance out what she is feeling.

Ian – Ian will feel angry because he is out of control of the situation and may become snappy with others. It isn't that he feels snappy. It's simply that he doesn't know any other way of expressing self-doubt and lack of control over his circumstances.

If you were to judge, you would probably say Mary is a leader. Susan is a plodder, and Ian is a grouch, but as you can see from the way each of them thinks, each, in turn, is using what they can to combat a difficult situation and should not be judged for it, other than using an understanding empathy for their circumstances.

When you consider that human physiology is the same for everyone, i.e., we need food, we need love, we need purpose, and we need good health, then you will also appreciate that each human being responds to life within the level of their own capacity and it's not for others to judge how they did. We can only guess how others will react to certain circumstances, but we can be more accurate in our assessment if we are empathetic and can place ourselves in the shoes of others. Mindfulness is all about taking judgment out of the equation. Perhaps you can start by forgiving. Forgive yourself for the things you can't do or that you failed in. Then forgive those around you who have seemingly wronged you. The point of forgiveness is to give you a fresh starting point, from which you will take judgment out of the picture. It frees you and allows your mind not to hold grudges or biases toward or against other people.

Now try this mindfulness exercise, which also combines a little neuro-linguistic therapy that helps you to drop all of your negative conceptions about things that have happened to you in your life. You can't change those things, and the more you think about them, the more they are allowed to anger you or hurt you, but the anger and hurt are self-inflicted by letting events from the past creep into this present moment. As you know, mindfulness is about this moment and no other. It does not look back, and it does not move forward by worrying about things that have not yet happened. Now add the neuro-linguistic bit, and you have a fine state of affairs, where you can control your feelings even more. Think for one moment about something that bugs you, and that makes you angry that has happened to you in the past. It may have to do with betrayal, or it may have to do with the parent-child dynamic. Now go to YouTube and find some circus music. What I want you to do is go from the present time and replay the event that happened to you, but this time play it backward and play the music at the same time. Close your eyes and think about everything winding backward that has to do with that event and see it as a movie-going in reverse. Then open your eyes and try to think about that event again. You will probably find that you can't really be hurt by it because you now associate it with the strangeness of playback. If this system works for you, do this before your next mindfulness meditation session. Start your session with a mind that is open to positivity instead of being filled with negative thoughts.

Mindfulness and Judgment

Chose a time when you know you will not be disturbed for a while and sit in a comfortable chair and focus your attention on something within that room, where you don't have to strain your neck to look at it. It should be something within your eye's reach and something that you can take your gaze back to as you go through this mindfulness session.

Start to breathe as you have done before: in through the nostrils to the count of eight and out to the count of ten. Smokers may find this hard to do since they tend to breathe through the mouth. However, it's important to use your nostrils because they filter and clean the air that you breathe; also, the air you breathe in through your nostrils is delivered into your body at the correct temperature. Stick with it and continue to breathe in this way. Now focus your eyes upon the object that you have chosen and keep on breathing in this way. If thoughts come to your mind, you must not judge them or allow them to form chains of thought. Instead of that, you need to banish them by simply going back into being in the moment and looking at whatever you have chosen as your focal point.

What I want you to do immediately after you have done this for ten minutes is to write down the thoughts that invaded your mind while you were doing this. The fact is that we have thoughts for a specific purpose, and I would never suggest ignoring those thoughts to the extent that you ignore your life obligations, and some of those thoughts may have been important to you. Look at those thoughts.

- Which are negative thoughts?
- Which were unnecessary thoughts?
- Which thoughts involved judgment?
- Which thoughts were reminders?

Now go about your normal day and act on those thoughts that were necessary, but what you are doing is beginning to recognize the pattern of thoughts that come to your head, and you will soon realize which thoughts are necessary ones and act on them and which were superfluous. I am leading you up to meditation in a very slow way intentionally. If you are someone who suffers from anger and who wants anger management, then it's not a good idea to just try meditating. You will lose patience with yourself and will give up. Thus, these exercises help you to see the process before you do it so that when you actually meditate, you will understand what's going on in your mind.

Exercise in Self-Control

In this exercise, look back at your memories for a moment. Sit down and write the things that you have found hard to forgive in your life. Then go through them and find a way to come to terms with each of them without using any type of judgment. For example, if your list says:

- My wife hurt me when she left
- My children have not stayed in touch enough
- My work is boring

Look at each of these and sincerely mean what you say when you forgive each one of the situations.

- I forgive my wife and will get on with my life
- My children have lives of their own, and I forgive them
- I forgive myself for not being in work that makes me happy

I know that someone who is angry finds it hard to forgive, but the moment that you do, and truly believe in your sincerity, you free your mind from negativity and judgment. Forgiveness makes you a nicer person, someone your wife/husband may like more or your children may want to visit. You cannot hope to move on while your thoughts are planted in the past, and that's what mindfulness is all about. Do you know how unattractive angry people are? Stop being angry and start forgiving. Stop judging and start seeing that other people have their motives for doing what they do, and you will become a more positive person.

The law of attraction dictates that positive people act as magnets for other positive people, but it works the other way around too. Let's look at how negative you could be to others through your anger:

You are angry at your child – Thus your child fears you. Fear is negative and unhelpful.

You are angry at your wife – Your wife fears you – Love cannot be based upon fear.

You are angry at your neighbor – Your neighbor is angry at you – two negatives do not make a positive.

The whole point is that anger and negativity breeds anger, frustration, and negativity, and you surround yourself with it the whole time that you hold onto grudges and cannot let go of past events. Mindfulness is about this moment in time. It's about using all of your senses to enjoy this moment in time, and it's not conditional upon anything being joyful yesterday or unhappy yesterday. It's an opportunity to view the world in a different way. Now let's try something different with the people you are angry toward.

Instead of showing anger, show friendliness, but it must be genuine.

Instead of being angry with your child, encourage your child to be himself.

Instead of harboring anger at your partner, encourage your partner to succeed in whatever they want to do.

The law of attraction will make you look a whole lot more attractive to those people than anger ever will. On the way to work today, smile at a few people. That doesn't mean giving them a leering grin. It simply means giving them a smile of encouragement and see what happens. People at work will treat you better. People in the street who are total strangers will react in a more positive way, and being present at the moment and smiling can change your whole outlook and your future. Move from one moment to the next, thinking only about that moment that you are in. There is a saying that you need to "stop and smell the roses," and what that means is that often our minds are so occupied with all of the negative things going on that we don't notice things around us that our senses should be enjoying. People walk through a park without even looking at the flowers. People walk down a street, looking into their phones and don't even really know what the weather is doing because they are too preoccupied with other things. Start to be present in your life, instead of being absent due to your thoughts being elsewhere.

How Blame Works

Sara and John's house caught on fire. Of course, everyone wanted to know what was to blame for the house fire. John wanted to know if Sara had left electrical items plugged in as he had always told her to unplug them when not in use. Sara wanted to know if John had sneaked down to the garage for a cigarette. The firemen wanted to know because if someone was made to blame for the fire, perhaps Sara and John could claim on the insurance of that person. Perhaps an electrician messed up. Perhaps there was a faulty gas appliance. While the work of the firefighters is pretty obviously intended to help people to avoid such things again, the blame of Sara and John toward each other is fruitless. They had lost their homes. If John had been the cause through a cigarette, do you think he did it on purpose? If Sara had left something plugged in, do you not think that she knows it and regrets it? The point here is that blame is used to divert attention away from what really happened and serves very little purpose, especially personal blame between one person and another. When mistakes are made, people usually know that they have made them. They feel bad and learn from those mistakes not to do the same things again. If you cannot forgive them, you need to understand that it's not your place to forgive them. It's your place to support them through the horrors of such a situation and to learn something from it. The consequences of the fire in the hypothetical case are that the couple lost their home. No amount of blame can change that and it's the same in most cases where blame is employed.

I want to tell you about a situation I encountered in my youth. In one office where I worked, I made a terrible beginner error, which threw the computers in the office into a situation of chaos. I was afraid I would be fired, but instead of that, my boss called me into the office and discussed what we could all do together to fix the problem. There was no blame attached to it, but what came out of my mistake was regret on my part and a huge willingness to try and find solutions. The solidarity in the office was amazing because no one blamed anyone, and no one made anyone else feel ashamed in front of others. They simply worked together to put it right and what I learned in those moments of despair was that my boss already knew I was sorry and prolonging that misery was not the right way forward. Instead, he chose to go through the error with me and help me and others to put it right. Blame serves no purpose.

What I want you to do is to look through your life at people you blame and learn some way to move forward and forgive without judgment. It's quite hard for someone who suffers from anger to do, but when they do it, it frees the mind of that negative attitude, and it makes people feel happier to move forward. You may not have thought about it, but perhaps there are people who show negative attitudes toward you. They hold themselves back, so instead of being upset by it, be compassionate, and know that the only person suffering from that blame is the person feeling it. Let go of judgment and liberate yourself from the burden of the weight of negativity.

I had to devote a whole chapter to this because one of the most important lessons you learn from mindfulness is that letting go is your road to liberation and you can't really do that unless you have examined your thoughts and biases and learned to move forward before you try to tackle becoming mindful of the present time and making the most of it.

Chapter Fifteen

What Should You Expect of Yourself During Meditation?

If you go in for a race and you cross the final line, you achieve something. The trouble is that people want gratification, and the gratification that comes from mindfulness isn't sudden, so you are not going to see any kind of prize at the end of each session of mindfulness. What you will see, however, is a change in your attitude, and that's a true prize because it's something that can last a lifetime. These are some of the things that you will notice about your behavior toward others:

- You will become more patient

- You will listen more than talk

- You will not get as angry

- You will find yourself more in control of your life

One of the most wonderful things about mindfulness is that it affects you all of the time. However, when you go through the mindfulness meditation exercise daily, you will come across the following frustrations:

- I can't get things out of my mind

- I don't feel like I am achieving anything
- I find my mind wanders
- I have trouble keeping the breathing to time
- I am not sure I am cut out for this

The reason I emphasize all these things is that during the meditation process, you should have no expectations of yourself. When you go on a diet, you expect to lose weight, and the sooner, the better. Humans have started to depend upon instant gratification, and meditation isn't like that. There are no prizes if you get it right. There are no instant feelings of winning at all, but what you don't know is that you are a winner long term. Over the term of your life, while you meditate, things are changing within your brain, and it is these things that will contribute to your ability to live life without anger.

Don't expect badges or prizes. The badges and prizes are something you can give yourself if you want to see your progress, but what will happen is that you will begin to feel more mellow, and that will help you to relate to the people around you. That's the prize. YOU become easier to live with. People around you appreciate you more, and you actually get to like who you are. That's a huge prize, but it's not instant gratification. If you are looking for instant gratification, then meditation isn't going to give it to you. You can keep a note of your progress if you want to and use the moments after you meditate to make notes of things you feel you can change to make tomorrow's session even better.

For example, if you noticed that there was a draft from the window that distracted you, this can remind you to reposition your cushion so that you don't have that draft tomorrow. Or, if you found that you were obsessed with a certain thought, you can persuade yourself that you will empty your mind and not give this thought credence while you are meditating.

Meditation will make you stronger and happier long term, so try to keep at it. It's a daily event because what you are trying to achieve is instilling the habit into the hippocampus sufficiently so that you do it without even having to think about it each day, as a habit. When you suddenly find yourself at the end of a meditation session, and you don't even remember starting it, then you can tell yourself you are on the right track, that your subconscious mind has actually grabbed the idea that this is something you are going to do on a daily basis.

Mindfulness meditation and mindfulness practice make you feel differently about yourself and about others. It also makes you more patient and less angry because you start to see things from other people's perspectives and can be more helpful to them and mindful of their difficulties.

So if you suffer from any of the expected feelings about your meditation, keep on regardless because you will notice the improvements when you are least expecting them. In fact, many people who have tried mindfulness have been surprised by the changes that it makes in their lives, as can be witnessed in the case of Sara Lazar, who approached it with skepticism too. Remember that mindfulness in total is not just about meditation. It is far more wide-reaching, as you will have learned through the process of this book.

Be patient with yourself until you see a difference because it will happen. It is a natural follow on from a mindful approach. If you need further proof of this, you may be interested to know that medical scientists have been working with the Dalai Lama, looking for solutions to problems in today's world. As a direct result of this, mindfulness has been used to help people with all kinds of problems, instead of falling back on modern medications. It is longer lasting, and it changes the approach of the individual to life so that problems do not repeat themselves in the future. Mindfulness is strengthening you and changing your fundamental approach to life, so once you think and act in a mindful way, anger is no longer a part of who you are. You are much more likely to find solutions by other means.

Chapter Sixteen

Self-Love and Respect from Mindfulness

Many people who have picked up this book or read the introduction may feel that mindfulness is one of those new-fangled belief systems that doesn't really relate to their lives. Look at the Maslow model of what human beings need in their lives and you will find that apart from the obvious, like food and shelter, you also need all of the elements listed in the hierarchy of needs that Maslow created as a model to help people to reach self-realization or to become the best person they can become. You know yourself that you have anger problems, so where on the scale does that come into the picture?

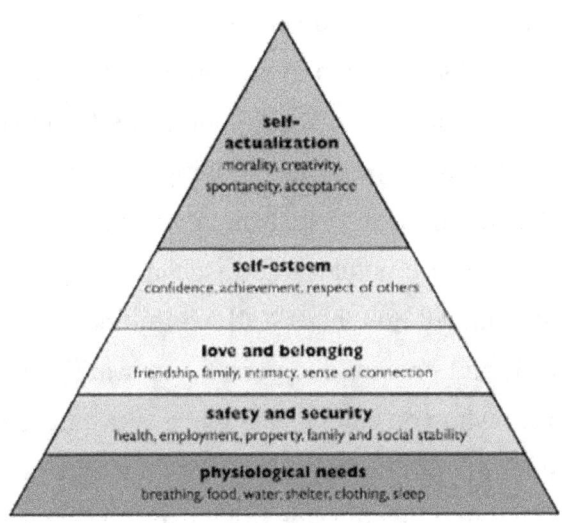

We know that you need food and shelter and perhaps even need the work that you do and purpose in life. You also need to make yourself as safe as you can and feel secure about life. Love and belonging come next on the scale, and people who are always angry and unlikely to love themselves very much at all. In fact, mindfulness helps you to build that part of your life so that you can equally give respect and love and receive it because you become more worthy of it when you have your anger under control.

Mindfulness helps you to relate to others. It shows you the world as you should see it rather than simply seeing your own point of view. When you are so narrow-minded as to think that your view is the only one that matters, it's unlikely that you will be able to relate to others to even make friends. Thus, to gain the love and belonging that you need, mindfulness will help you to be more aware of your actions, your interactions, and your relationships with other people.

So then we find the area called self-esteem. Do you think that you are a good person? Do you think that your anger serves any kind of purpose to make you feel good about yourself? Of course, you don't. Otherwise, why would you be looking for solutions? Well, mindfulness has an answer to that dilemma, too, because through silencing the mind, you actually get a chance to go back to core learning about yourself, and that's well worth it because it helps you to build yourself and become the person you want to be. There are no restrictions in who you can be, and when you start to be aware of the positive sides of your character, you begin to like yourself more. Certainly, you will not like the side of yourself that gets angry, but if you use mindfulness, you will begin to like the side of you that can resist anger.

The top layer on Maslow Hierarchy of human needs is self-actualization. What does this mean? Well, it means reaching your best. You cannot possibly feel that you have reached your best when you are brought back to earth with a thump by your own anger. Anger is a lack of control. It's negative. You already know that it hurts those around you, but it does far more damage to your long term. People who are perpetually angry often don't like themselves, so they can never really reach the peaks of self-actualization. This is the point where you find that you are happy with who you are – regardless of human flaws – and where you feel you have reached the pinnacle of understanding your life and being happy with it.

If you take a look around you at unhappy people, there will always be a cause for that unhappiness, and it will always be something that is shown on the Maslow Hierarchy of needs. For example, a homeless person who cannot feed her children will not have all of her needs met, and this is because her basic physiological needs are not being met. Someone else who has no friends will not find happiness because part of the Maslow model demands that a human being has human connections and acceptance of others as part of the road toward happiness. The reason I use this model to demonstrate the way that life works are because you may need a little additional fuel to your fire to make you take action and take the mindfulness route seriously. It isn't just the people who thought up mindfulness that would use these methods to improve their lives, as can be seen by the Maslow model. You need all of these attributes to find human happiness and mindfulness helps you to find them.

When you learn to empty the mind of the things that are of no consequence to you, you have a greater capacity to find solutions to problems that may otherwise have caused you anger. Imagine the fullness of the mind in this modern day and age, and there is little wonder that people get upset. Their minds are filled with everything they have seen on the TV, internet, as well as thoughts about work, about relationships, achievements and thoughts about society in general, not to mention expectations of self and of others. Good grief, there's no wonder that so many millions of people all over the world are seeking help with their mental health problems. So, losing your temper and not being able to manage your anger is just the tip of the iceberg. Mindfulness helps you to empty out all of the things that really don't matter and begin to recognize those that do matter. You no longer feel that you have to keep up with others, but because of this lack of self-expectation, you can usually manage to excel them rather than merely keep up. When you empty your mind of all of the clutter that builds up through your life, your priorities change. You are able to see the full picture, and you take care of all of the needs shown on the Maslow model through your mindfulness.

People often think that the word mindfulness depicts an image of a mind that is full when, in fact, the reverse is the truth. When your mind is empty of the frivolities of life that don't matter, you can think more clearly. It doesn't mean that you can't have fun. In fact, you will find this lightheartedness that you feel is part and parcel of mindfulness as you become more aware of people around you, and even your kids can show you how to have fun if you are open-minded enough to let them guide you simply. You can also find your creative route in life; your brain is less charged up with all the false promises of the adverts or the expectations you felt that you had to live up to. The fact is that the only expectations that matter are at this moment. I expect at this moment that I will reach over and grab my coffee and thoroughly enjoy it. That's what life is. It's a series of moments, and somehow people who demonstrate anger have forgotten that anger serves no purpose. It doesn't correct errors, and it creates negativity and can even hurt others long term.

I remember discussing something that a child did with his parents. The child had stolen something, but he couldn't understand why the child needed to do that. The fact was that the boy was searching for attention, and the only time that he got his father's attention was when he did something wrong. At all other times, his father was too busy working or competing with the world. When he realized his error, he started spending more time with his child, but the consequences of not changing would have been drastic. For example, his child would only have had negative memories of his father when he grew older. He wouldn't know his father was capable of fun. Life passes too quickly, and the guy I was talking to was only beginning to learn mindfulness. When he understood the error of his ways, he told his son, and they talked about ways in which they could spend more time together and stop all the anger in its tracks. Children teach us a lot about life but parents who don't look for those lessons learn very little. Mindfulness helps you to stop and see what's painfully obvious to a child. The child has not yet been spoiled by society's perception of how a human being should be, and children are much more mindful in their approach to life than adults are. In many countries, children are included in meditation sessions, and they are much more receptive than adults and are able to use this to calm their worries and to become much more self-confident.

In the western world, we have not yet reached that stage, but it's a good idea to start your mindfulness journey now because everyone around you will benefit from your mindful approach. Not only will you make your own life happier, but you will also contribute to the happiness of others. That's a wonderful goal, isn't it and helps you to work toward what Maslow says is the highest aim of human beings in their plight for happiness. You can realize so much if you run through the categories that Maslow believed contributed to human happiness and then try to tick the boxes on those areas where you are happy within your own life and work on areas that you feel are weak. As someone who is trying anger-management, the likely placers you lack are in human relationships with others and with your self-esteem. Work on these through mindfulness, and the rest will fall into place on its own.

There is so much for you to enjoy when you are able to forgive yourself and others for things that they may have done. When you hold grudges, you are stepping in the muddy ground, and you can't really find a stronghold. However, when you are able to let go and forgive, through mindful practices, you will find that you like yourself more and can relate to others in a much friendlier way.

Forgive them their lack of ability to drop grudges too because it isn't your weakness. It is theirs.

I hope that this chapter has helped to persuade you that there is some merit to the advice of experts who say that mindfulness can help your life in many different ways. Even Maslow agreed with this principle; all the areas touched upon are those that you aim for when you begin the journey to mindfulness.

Conclusion

I know that when you began to read this book, you were skeptical about what mindfulness could do to help you to overcome your anger issues. By now, you should have realized that mindfulness does require your input and action. It means changing your approach to life, and any person can do that with the willingness to change. Mindfulness does more than that, though. It changes your values, and it makes you a happier person because you begin to understand the link between you and the universe. You also expect change and make the most of each moment in your life because you know if you don't, you don't get a second chance at it. This moment is the most important moment of your life because it's the only moment that matters. What you do in one moment affects the next and the next and so forth, so being present in the moment is to your advantage.

There are many exercises within this book – some of which may seem like hard work, while others seem fun to try out with your family. However, you need to ask yourself why you came to look at this book in the first place to give you the motivation to make a difference. Anger eats away at you. I once tried to demonstrate this to someone who felt angry with his sister. Did his sister suffer from that anger? His sister lived many miles away and was probably unaware of his anger while he continued to hold grudges, and these grudges began to eat into the quality of his life. His sister was unaware of his anger toward her; she didn't suffer at all because she was too busy living her life. You have to accept that anger doesn't eat away at those to whom it is directed, although it can affect them, especially if the anger makes that person feel any form of lack of self-esteem. However, anger, in general, has more effect on the person who is exhibiting it. For many years, I believed that the anger I experienced as a child was responsible for the way I approached life, and although it played a part, I had to eventually accept that it was my perception of that event that was warped toward disappointment, self-esteem issues and even blaming someone from my past for the part they played in my anguish. It was only a little situation and nothing of any significance to anyone except me, as I learned much later in life, and in fact, I had fabricated my version of something that happened years before. The chances are that much of what makes you angry doesn't even really exist anymore. Sometimes it is a clash of perspectives, and that's all it is.

Mindfulness helps you to forget about the past and move on, insofar as building your own persona. It's much more powerful than holding onto the past and using it as an excuse not to develop. Blame is fruitless. It doesn't make anything better and comes about as a result of the judgment. You judge that someone else made you angry. The fact is that your perception of that event made you angry. What happens when you study mindfulness is that you drop that judgment, so it no longer plays that negative role in your life. You start to embrace diversity more and can see things from many perspectives, which makes you more powerful, rather than less powerful. It helps you to develop as a human being, and although the first few stumbling steps into mindfulness may appear to be doing nothing, don't believe it. It will work and does work, and the more you practice it, the more it helps you to change certain things about yourself and your relationship with the world around you:

- You will feel healthier
- You will make healthier choices
- You will enjoy life more
- You will be more aware of others
- You will not judge people
- You will not be afraid of other people's judgment

These are very powerful motivations to carry on practicing mindfulness, especially in this day and age.

I would suggest that you go back through the pages of the book and carry out the exercises that have been designed to introduce you to mindfulness. If they involve others, get your family or friends involved. Keep an open mind as you begin mindfulness meditation. An open mind is quite an important part of mindfulness, so make sure that you learn the breathing methods you have been shown in this book, as these will help you in the early days of trying to control your anger. Anger management has never been this easy. It is open to everyone who wants to try mindfulness, and you can even bring up your kids to be mindful, by sitting down and observing what's going on in the world, either in nature or by sharing information that is relevant to this moment. Give them the opportunity to view the world from another perspective.

Anger management means that you also need to address your wrongdoing. If you know that you have affected the lives of other people because of your temper, then it's not a bad idea to let those people know that you meant no offense. When you do this, it helps you to be more mindful in the future when it comes to responding to situations and triggers that start that feeling of needing to vent. Breathe, think things through, and be in the moment, rather than always looking at life through retrospect or anticipating it before it happens. When you learn the mindful way to deal with life, anger will have gone, and you will have become a better person for it.

References

What happens when you lose your temper?

https://www.medicalnewstoday.com/articles/190522.php#1

How Meditation Can Reshape Our Brains: Sara Lazar at TEDxCambridge 2011

https://www.youtube.com/watch?v=m8rRzTtP7Tc

www.ingramcontent.com/pod-product-compliance
Lightning Source LLC
Chambersburg PA
CBHW071524080526
44588CB00011B/1555